Our World in Focus

Moving Toward a Sustainable Future

ESSAYS | PHOTOGRAPHS | FACTS

OUR WORLD IN FOCUS: MOVING TOWARD A SUSTAINABLE FUTURE
FIRST PUBLISHED IN GREAT BRITAIN IN 2002 BY VISION ON PUBLISHING
AND EARTH PLEDGE FOUNDATION

VISION ON PUBLISHING
112-116 OLD STREET
LONDON EC1V 9BG
T: +44 (0)20 7549 6815
F: +44 (0)20 7336 0966
E: INFO@VISIONONPUBLISHING.COM
WWW.VOBOOKS.COM

EARTH PLEDGE FOUNDATION
122 EAST 38TH STREET
NEW YORK, NY 10016
T: +1 (212)725 6611
F: +1 (212)725 6774
WWW.EARTHPLEDGE.ORG

PHOTOGRAPHS © PHOTOGRAPHERS AS LISTED/MAGNUM PHOTOS
2002 DANNIELLE HAYES
2002 TIMOTHY HURSLEY
2002 SARAH OEHL
2002 JARRET SCHECTER

THE RIGHT OF EACH PHOTOGRAPHER AS LISTED TO BE IDENTIFIED AS THE AUTHOR
OF HIS OR HER WORK HAS BEEN ASSERTED BY HIM OR HER IN ACCORDANCE WITH
THE COPYRIGHT, DESIGNS AND PATENTS ACT OF 1988.

TYPOGRAPHY BUERO NEW YORK

ISBN 1 903399 68 8

REPROGRAPHICS AJD COLOR LTD
PRINTED IN ITALY

O*ur World in Focus* is an ambitious book that, through some striking and thought-provoking photographs and penetrating essays of renowned people, highlights the current state of humankind's relationship with the Earth and poses the question "Where do we go from here?"

This book is the brainchild of the Earth Pledge Foundation, a nonprofit organization established in 1991 by Theodore W. Kheel in support of the Rio Earth Summit. Ever since its inception, Earth Pledge has been at the forefront of innovative educational and media endeavors, mainstreaming the message of sustainability to key audiences. At a time when heads of state and most of the world's governments will be reviewing the progress—or lack thereof—in sustainable development since 1992, Earth Pledge lends its support to the World Summit in a most striking manner: by presenting "the state of the world" through photographs. The reader embarks on a journey that offers insight into humanity's most pressing issues and compelling innovations that address them.

Sustainability gives us the best chance we have to guarantee a secure future for our children. It offers a vision reflected in the large number of local projects and community initiatives that successfully combine social, economic, and environmental imperatives into a coherent whole. It is a vision based on the potential of new technologies that work with rather than against the local environment. It rests on an ethic of solidarity and responsibility to one another and to future generations. Every day, this vision gains in public, private, and social support; and together, through political will, practical steps, and partnerships, we can achieve what the vision promises.

Our World in Focus reaches out—by way of accessible artistic expression—to every citizen of the global village so that we all may connect to the essential endeavor of sustainability. Were we to succeed, would it not be a worthwhile legacy to be remembered as those who finally steered things right?

NITIN DESAI
SECRETARY-GENERAL OF THE UNITED NATIONS WORLD SUMMIT ON SUSTAINABLE DEVELOPMENT

In the late 1930s, the great American wilderness photographer Ansel Adams was commissioned to work on a limited-edition book project entitled *Sierra Nevada: The John Muir Trail*. His assignment coincided with a campaign to create King's Canyon National Park, located in the southern Sierra Nevadas, in California. Adams's photographs were instrumental in President Franklin Roosevelt's decision to incorporate King's Canyon into the national park system. It was an exquisite triumph for both artist and nature.

Great achievements can occur when art and politics come together to inspire social, cultural, and environmental change. The power of the arts to move people to action is limitless. This notion, central to Earth Pledge Foundation's history, is at the heart of our mission. It propels us to produce and support efforts that motivate social action.

Earth Pledge Foundation originated as a United Nations committee chaired by the influential New York City lawyer Theodore W. Kheel. Kheel, who served Presidents Kennedy, Johnson, and Ford as a mediator in major national labor disputes, wanted to encourage interest in the 1992 Earth Summit in Rio. To aid him in his efforts, Kheel enlisted the support of his friend, the internationally acclaimed artist Robert Rauschenberg, who created *Last Turn, Your Turn* (1991), the official artwork of the Earth Summit.

Since 1993, Earth Pledge has promoted sustainable lifestyle by highlighting the connection between everyday choices, personal well-being, and a healthy world. Our primary approach is to develop creative educational projects that offer sustainable solutions to professionals and the public.

Our World in Focus: Moving Toward a Sustainable Future presents photographs from a remarkable team of international photographers, the majority of whom are with the prestigious cooperative agency Magnum Photos. Together with a diverse array of authoritative voices—from the candid testimony of a young African woman to the insight of His Holiness the Dalai Lama—their work addresses key aspects of human experience: people, nature, food, shelter, community, pleasure, tragedy, economy, and progress.

Our planet is fragile, our demands great, and at the dawn of the 21st century, with ever increasing needs for food, water, shelter, sanitation, energy, health care, and security, we must strike an appropriate balance between economic growth and the preservation of social, cultural, and environmental systems.

In August 2002, the World Summit on Sustainable Development will be held in Johannesburg, South Africa, to devise new strategies for achieving Agenda 21, a global sustainable development action plan created at the Earth Summit. Tens of thousands of participants, including heads of state and government, national delegates, and leaders from nongovernmental organizations, businesses, and other major groups, will come together to formulate solutions to difficult global challenges.

Clearly, globalization has brought us closer to one another. We are now connected in ways that only a few generations back would have seemed the workings of witchcraft, the impact of which we can barely grasp. Nonetheless, 20 percent of the world's population consumes 70 to 80 percent of the world's resources. And while there is enough food to feed the world's people, 800 million are going hungry and 20,000 die each day of hunger-related diseases.

We are facing many difficulties, but we are also making phenomenal progress. The rate of HIV infection in Uganda is decreasing. Fuel cell technology has begun powering cars, vending machines, vacuum cleaners, and highway road signs. Although there is still great cause for concern, the concentration of ozone-depleting chlorofluorocarbons has declined in the lower atmosphere. The inhabitants of pioneering cities in England, Japan, and the United States are fishing in newly cleaned rivers and bays. A woman in Senegal is making soap out of an indigenous cereal crop to reduce soil erosion and earn a living. A design/build architecture program is bringing students to the impoverished rural American South to construct homes and community spaces—using donated and sustainable materials—for local families.

Much progress is being made in unexpected places. This is not a chance occurrence but the fruit of hard work, commitment, innovation, passion, and, above all, people's will. At every turn and in every country, dedicated groups, corporations, academics, governments, and enthusiastic individuals are making a difference.

For us, this book represents an opportunity to deliver awareness, ideas, inspiration, a sense of urgency, and useful knowledge to people around the globe. There are simple things we can all do to participate in assuring a sustainable future. From supporting local agriculture by purchasing food from nearby farmers to choosing products made from recycled and renewable materials, we can have a positive impact. Taking responsibility is vital to our success.

LESLIE HOFFMAN
EXECUTIVE DIRECTOR, EARTH PLEDGE FOUNDATION

CONTENTS

People

BEATRICE BIIRA
A STUDENT IN KAMPALA, UGANDA

As people we share a wide variety of universal experience, and throughout the world we live vastly different lives. Still, we have many of the same basic problems. Our faces reflect a far-reaching range of lifestyle, race, religion, taste, environment, culture, and class. What I find fascinating are the common threads that bind us.

My name is Beatrice Biira. I am an 18-year-old Ugandan woman. My family belongs to the Bakonzo tribe from western Uganda. I attend a girls' boarding school in Kampala, my country's capital, where there are girls from all over Africa, of different tribes and languages. I have been to many places within Uganda. I have also traveled to Rwanda and to the U.S.A.

For over half my life, a civil war has raged in my country between the Lord's Resistance Army, under rebel leader Joseph Kony, and the Ugandan government. At the core of this conflict is a lack of patriotic unity among the nationals and a fight for political power. This war has robbed so many dear lives in the affected areas. All over the world, there is persistent armed conflict.

Conflict is just one of the major issues faced by humanity; but there is also poverty, inequality, discrimination, and disease. Though our challenges bring suffering, they serve to give us an understanding of one another's plight and hence offer us the opportunity to find commonality and connection as people.

How can we preserve human cultures while making progress? Simply defined, culture is a collection of the traditional ways of doing things. All over the world, through sayings, legends, and songs, we connect to our culture, which gives us a sense of belonging. Every society has a culture that is highly valued. Some cultural practices, however, prevent people from progressing. Take, for example, the practice of female circumcision among the Kikuyu in Kenya and the Sebei in Uganda. Though thankfully declining, this sheer violence and abuse of the human body still exists, yet the participants see nothing wrong with it. Education can bring awareness of the dangers of some cultural practices and the importance of preserving those at risk of being lost.

In thinking about conflict, culture, and other universally shared needs and experiences, I believe that education wields a priceless power. In Uganda, sending girls to school has not yet been widely culturally accepted. We wage serious campaigns for girl-child education; it has empowered women in Uganda and enabled them to participate in the development of Uganda. Through education, we have had the opportunity to elevate our status while maintaining our beloved cultural practices. Uganda's vice president is a very powerful woman.

Consider those who have no access to education because of financial reasons. In my school, I pay fees equivalent to $650 annually. What about that rurally based peasant father who earns $10 a month after marketing all his hard-earned produce? He is often the sole provider for his ten-member family. These are disadvantaged people who do not choose to live under such circumstances.

As human beings with life in us, we laugh when happy, we get excited, we get scared and hurt, the same red blood flows out of our veins when we are injured, we respire, and we all die. We have the same basic needs for love, clothing, shelter, food, and care. Throughout our lives, we grow mentally, physically, and emotionally. Our ideas, knowledge, and exposure differ, but our instincts are the same. If a president of some nation, a miner, a peasant farmer, a priest, and a pilot were stranded together in a desert, their first instinct would be survival, irrespective of their origin, race, color, and status. They would all look for water to quench their fiery thirst.

Once we develop an understanding that as people we are actually the same, we need to develop human hearts for one another. Many countries are antagonistic. Poverty, hunger, violation, war, disease, and more have perpetually deprived the world of many dear lives. The root cause for all these is conflict and war.

Since we are all human, then let us be human. The only way to make the world a better place for happy people is through unity and love for one another as God's creations and as people. As I write this essay, I am dreaming about a peaceful and calm world with united and smiling faces of people.

PALESTINIANS MAKE UP

THE SINGLE LARGEST GROUP OF refugees,

TOTALING 4 MILLION PEOPLE.

_ KERALA **INDIA** CROWD ATTENDING THE ELEPHANT MARCH

_ ONTARIO **CANADA** MOTHER AND DAUGHTER

_ KERALA **INDIA** CROWD ATTENDING THE ELEPHANT MARCH

_ LONDON **ENGLAND** LONDON UNDERGROUND

_ LIBYA-NIGER BORDER ILLEGAL IMMIGRANTS FLEEING THEIR HOMELANDS

_ ONTARIO **CANADA** MOTHER AND DAUGHTER

505 MILLION PEOPLE LIVE IN COUNTRIES THAT ARE

water stressed OR WATER SCARCE; THAT FIGURE

IS EXPECTED TO BE BETWEEN 2.4 BILLION AND 3.4 BILLION BY 2025.

_ WAMENA **INDONESIA** DANI TRIBESMAN ACCOMPANYING DAUGHTER TO SCHOOL

_ ATLANTA GEORGIA **U.S.A.** PARALYMPICS

22

_ **SLOVAKIA** ROMA PEOPLE CELEBRATING THE NEW YEAR

AN ESTIMATED 800 MILLION SMOKERS—

70% OF THE WORLD'S TOTAL—NOW LIVE IN

DEVELOPING COUNTRIES ALONG WITH

countless PASSIVE SMOKERS

WHO SHARE THE RISKS OF SMOKING-RELATED DISEASES.

EACH DAY, SOME HUNDRED THOUSAND YOUNG PEOPLE

BECOME REGULAR LONG-TERM SMOKERS.

_ WINDSOR **ENGLAND** POLO TOURNAMENT

_ LAKELAND FLORIDA **U.S.A.** YOUNG PAGEANT WINNER

_ TAOS NEW MEXICO **U.S.A.** NATIVE AMERICAN AT A POWWOW

_ NEW YORK CITY **U.S.A.** BIRTHDAY CELEBRATION

_ LONDON **ENGLAND** MIXED MUSLIM PRIMARY SCHOOL

OF EVERY 100 CHILDREN born IN 2000, 26 WILL NOT BE

IMMUNIZED AGAINST PREVENTABLE CHILDHOOD ILLNESSES,

30 WILL SUFFER FROM MALNUTRITION IN THEIR FIRST FIVE YEARS,

AND 17 WILL NEVER GO TO SCHOOL.

_ NEW YORK CITY **U.S.A.** URBAN TEENAGERS

_ ROATAN **HONDURAS** FATHER AND DAUGHTER AT HOME

_ SAN JUAN ATILAN **GUATEMALA** MAYA MEN

_ ROATAN **HONDURAS** FATHER AND DAUGHTER AT HOME

_ DEIR EL ADRA **EGYPT** COPT VILLAGE NEAR MINYA

_ TAHOUA **NIGER** WOMAN AND CHILD FROM THE NOMADIC BOROROS "PEULS" TRIBE

_ SAN JUAN ATILAN **GUATEMALA** MAYA MEN

_ HAVANA **CUBA** WEDDING DAY

_ **BERING STRAIT** LOCAL SHAMAN

_ LHASA **TIBET** JOKHANG SQUARE

_ DAKAR **SENEGAL** VEGETABLE SELLER

_ **JAPAN** TWO WOMEN IN TRADITIONAL CLOTHING

Nature

DR. THOMAS E. LOVEJOY
PRESIDENT OF THE HEINZ CENTER, U.S.A.

Human beings came into existence as but a single species among millions of other animals, plants, and microorganisms. Over the course of our history our species has distinguished itself from our fellow living things through our ability to alter the carrying capacity of the environment for our own benefit. Sometimes we increase the carrying capacity: for example, through the invention of agriculture at the time of the Neolithic revolution. In other cases we reduce it, as by lowering fish stocks through overfishing. Less obvious are the indirect ways in which we lower the carrying capacity—through the extinction of species, for example, or by missing an opportunity to discover a beneficial new drug because resources were lost.

The diversity of life, commonly referred to as biodiversity, contributes in countless ways to our daily lives. From timber to truffles, through direct harvest from nature, we acquire an astonishing variety of "goods." In this regard, pharmaceuticals are noteworthy. Curare, for instance, extracted from new-world tropical forests, is used as a muscle relaxant in major abdominal surgery. Our ecosystems also provide "ecosystem services," be it through the provision of potable water by watersheds, the pollination of agricultural crops, or the work of soil microbes that generate soil fertility.

A first estimate of the value of ecosystem services puts it at tens of trillions of dollars annually for the globe. New York City recently found it more economical (by a factor of ten) to restore the ecosystem service value of its watershed by restoring biodiversity rather than by building a water-treatment plant at ten times the cost. Costa Rica now has a law encouraging payments to private landholders for ecological services rendered. This conscious effort on the part of a government to incentivize the public deserves applause. We need much more of this kind of action.

In 1992, at the Earth Summit in Rio, the nations of the world created the Convention on Biological Diversity with the dual purpose of conserving our seriously endangered biological resources and regulating their uses and benefits in an equitable way among nations. Undoubtedly, both conservation and some of the questions relating to use and benefit sharing have made advances since—but not as much as was hoped or is needed.

Now, as we head toward the 2002 World Summit on Sustainable Development in Johannesburg, many are concerned that the environment is likely to be ignored in an almost exclusive focus on the social, economic, and poverty agendas. In the end, it is impossible, of course, to have sustainable development without a healthy environment, but the irreversible nature of extinction argues that biological diversity must not be left to later.

Throughout the planet are 25 terrestrial biological "hotspots" where large numbers of species that occur nowhere else survive for the moment. They do so despite increasing pressure. Recent scientific studies show that hotspots also exist in the two-thirds of Earth's surface occupied by marine ecosystems. These clearly represent priorities for conservation. There is a fundamental need for all landscapes to be biologically functional, that is, with their ecosystem services intact. Clearly, then, no shortage of challenges exists for the "green" agenda.

The natural world provides us with a metric for sustainability. Biological diversity can help measure sustainability and ensure that the environment does not take an inappropriate backseat to the social and economic elements. Basically, all environmental problems are "problems" because they affect living systems. Consequently, the biodiversity of a region, or lack thereof, reflects the full array of environmental problems that occur there.

As was first demonstrated in rivers in the late 1940s by ecologist Ruth Patrick, biology serves as a useful tool for assessing the impact of human activities on ecosystems. The Patrick principle will not necessarily reveal whether there are problems with the social and economic aspects of sustainability. Rather, if our activities are too unsustainable, that situation will reflect on the characteristic biological diversity of the region under examination.

The diversity of life is so wondrous and beautiful that conservation is important for this reason alone. There is no question that we are in the initial stages of what could become the sixth major extinction crisis in the history of life on Earth, the difference being that we are responsible and are capable of doing something about it. If we do not act, we will leave an impoverished and lonely planet to our descendants. We must not fail.

_ LAGUNAS **BOLIVIA** NATURAL HOT SPRINGS AND GEYSERS

_ **ANTARCTICA** GLACIAL SEAS

BECAUSE OF OF CLIMATE change, SEA LEVELS ARE

PROJECTED TO INCREASE FROM .09 M TO .88 M BY 2100,

CAUSING GRAVE NEGATIVE IMPACTS ON COASTAL COMMUNITIES.

_ **BRAZIL** SNAKE BASKING IN THE GRASSLANDS

_ NEW JERSEY **U.S.A** URBAN NATURE

_ NEAR MEXICO CITY **MEXICO** TREE ON A MOUNTAINTOP

_ WYOMING **U.S.A.** LODGEPOLE PINES AFTER THE 1988 FIRE IN YELLOWSTONE NATIONAL PARK

_ GALÁPAGOS ISLANDS **ECUADOR** TURTLES IN A WILDLIFE CONSERVATION RESERVE

BETWEEN 1970 AND 1995, HUMAN ACTIVITIES

DESTROYED 30% OF THE NATURAL WORLD. THE EARTH

WILL HAVE LOST 25% OF ITS species BY 2050.

_ **BURKINA FASO** RIVER NEAR THE NIGER BORDER

_ GAOTIAN GUILIN **CHINA** RICE PLANTATION

_ SARAWAK **MALAYSIA** DEER CAVE, MULU NATIONAL PARK

_ HODH **MAURITANIA** SUN SETTING OVER THE DESERT

_ DORSET **ENGLAND** HYDRANGEAS GROWING IN A SUBURBAN AREA

_ **KUWAIT** BIRD DYING IN AN OIL SPILL OFF THE COAST OF SAUDI ARABIA

_ KALIMANTAN **BORNEO** EX-CAPTIVE ORANGUTAN AT CAMP LEAKEY RESEARCH STATION

_ AIX-EN-PROVENCE **FRANCE** RURAL HOME GARDEN

WORLDWIDE, LESS THAN 10% OF TOTAL WASTE,

INCLUDING FARM RUNOFF, INDUSTRIAL POLLUTION,

AND HUMAN waste, IS TREATED BEFORE IT ENTERS

RIVERS THAT ARE USED FOR DRINKING, SANITATION,

IRRIGATION, OR INDUSTRY.

_ MOUNT PAEKTU **NORTH KOREA** PRISTINE WATERS OF LAKE OF HEAVEN

_ LANGUEDOC-ROUSSILLON **FRANCE** SIGEAN AFRICAN NATURE RESERVE

_ BIALOWIEZA **POLAND** BISON

_ BIALOWIEZA **POLAND** SILVER BIRCH TREES IN A FOREST RESERVE

_ SICILY **ITALY** LAVA FROM MOUNT ETNA BURNS THE FOREST

THE TOTAL CONSUMPTION OF

ozone-depleting

SUBSTANCES HAS FALLEN BY 85% AS A RESULT OF

DELIBERATE INTERNATIONAL COOPERATION.

_ MANILA **PHILIPPINES** ALLIGATOR FARM

Shelter

DR. KEN YEANG
ARCHITECT AND ECOLOGIST, U.K./MALAYSIA

Shelter starts closer than we think. It is essentially an extension of our clothing, providing us with another layer of enclosure between ourselves and the natural environment. But like clothing, it does more than protect us from the elements: it fulfills other human needs—for comfort, security, and privacy and for symbolic, aesthetic, and cultural connections.

The need for shelter is constant across all walks of life, yet its form shifts with every context, reflecting the endemic culture that has created it, which in turn is shaped by the geography and climate of a particular locale. "Shelter" can be as simple as a tree cover or as grand as a palace. It can be a shell, a cave, a nest, a shed, or a mall.

The roots of architecture are found in natural or primary dwellings, the "primitive hut." Architecture begins with the concept that buildings serve fundamentally as an environmental filter, mediating between our bodies and the often hostile external environment. It allows us to pursue our activities protected, in comfort and uninterrupted despite the vicissitudes of the climate outside.

The form, function, and expectations of these environmental filters naturally vary with climate and location. For instance, in cold zones, buildings must provide insulation from wind, snowstorms, or worse, whereas in the tropics, buildings may be more minimal, functioning as shields, mainly from sun or rain, but also, in some places, withstanding hazards such as typhoons and earthquakes.

Modern building technology has spoiled us to the extent that we expect a consistent comfort level. We have become less accustomed to extremes of heat and cold and less willing to modify our activities according to the weather outside. We now supplement our shelters with increasingly complex mechanical and electrical systems, generally using non-renewable energies to sustain and control our internal environments with high comfort thresholds. This unfortunately further disconnects us from nature.

Our disregard for context and urge to control our surroundings are exactly where our dislocations from nature begin, engendering an insensitivity about how we relate to the natural world, the biosphere. This tendency is perilous, for it multiplies. Unlike any other species in nature, humankind builds shelters and structures in large aggregations and on a large scale. We then link these to one another with roads and infrastructure. The result is an inorganic built environment, in the form of a callous imposition on the natural landscape that is paved, impervious, and predominantly artificial.

Buildings have ecological impacts that are deep and dramatic, that devastate and deplete the ecosystems of the very resources that make it habitable. Whereas our shelters began as forms within nature, drawing from nature, our built environment has become one of nature's worst threats. We might contend that this battle for a sustainable future will be won or lost in our cities, the apotheoses of our built environment.

Buildings encroach on nature: they disrupt, consume, and spoil it. They are responsible for up to 40 percent of all resource consumption and up to 45 percent of all non-renewable energy. They contribute 26 percent of waste to landfills and discharge waste, heat, and myriad pollutants. However, Earth's natural systems can withstand and assimilate only so much before the damage becomes irreparable. We urgently need to change this process and to find inventive ways to contribute positively through design.

In building more shelters to accommodate our ever growing population, we are in effect simplifying the biosphere and making it increasingly inorganic. In the process, we threaten biodiversity by destroying the natural habitats of other life-forms whose survival is crucial to our own. For our own survival, we must alter this trend and balance our present manmade environment's increasing artificiality by reintroducing more organic content to our surroundings. We need to "green" our built environments, literally, by integrating biotic landscape elements and greenery. In my own built works, that is just what we have done, taking advantage of the ability of vegetation to reduce the heat-island effect in the city, absorb storm water, and oxygenate the air. We must reverse the process of environmental simplification and rediscover the benefits of complexity and diversity in nature.

A shelter is like a prosthesis, an artificial limb or heart. A prosthesis must not only perform its particular task but at the same time be organically integrated with its host body. For buildings, the biosphere is the host organic body, and our built environment must be harmless additions, integrated with it systemically and seamlessly. Moreover, our shelters must be reusable, recyclable, and, at the end of their useful lives, restored to nature's cycles and systems—in other words, made useful from source to sink. These are the biggest design challenges confronting us today. Our buildings must again become whole with nature.

IF EVERY HOUSEHOLD IN THE UNITED STATES USED THE MOST EFFICIENT REFRIGERATORS

AVAILABLE, THE ELECTRICITY SAVED WOULD ELIMINATE the need

FOR MORE THAN 20 LARGE POWER PLANTS.

_ RHODES **GREECE** TRADITIONAL MEDITERRANEAN HOME

73

_ MIAMI FLORIDA **U.S.A.** FRUIT GROWING IN A SUBURBAN BACKYARD

_ NEW JERSEY **U.S.A.** LEAVING FOR WORK

_ JERUSALEM **ISRAEL** ULTRAMODERN HOUSING ESTATE

NEW YORK CITY PRODUCES 11,000 TONS OF *garbage* EACH DAY. FOR EVERY 40,000 TONS OF GARBAGE ADDED TO A LANDFILL, AT LEAST ONE ACRE OF LAND IS LOST TO FUTURE USE.

_ NEW YORK CITY **U.S.A.** MANHATTAN OFFICE BUILDING

_ TRINIDAD **CUBA** WORKHORSE KEPT ON PORCH OVERNIGHT

SINCE THE 1970s, green roofs, WHOSE SURFACES ARE SUBSTANTIALLY COVERED WITH VEGETATION, HAVE BECOME AN IMPORTANT PART OF THE EUROPEAN LANDSCAPE, WHERE THEY OCCUPY MORE THAN 100 MILLION SQUARE FEET OF ROOFTOP SPACE.

_ TASHKENT **UZBEKISTAN** MEN PRAYING AT A TRADITIONAL UZBEK WEDDING

_ HOITOTOS **COLOMBIA** INDIAN CHILD IN A RURAL HOME

_ GAO **MALI** TYPICAL MALI HOTEL

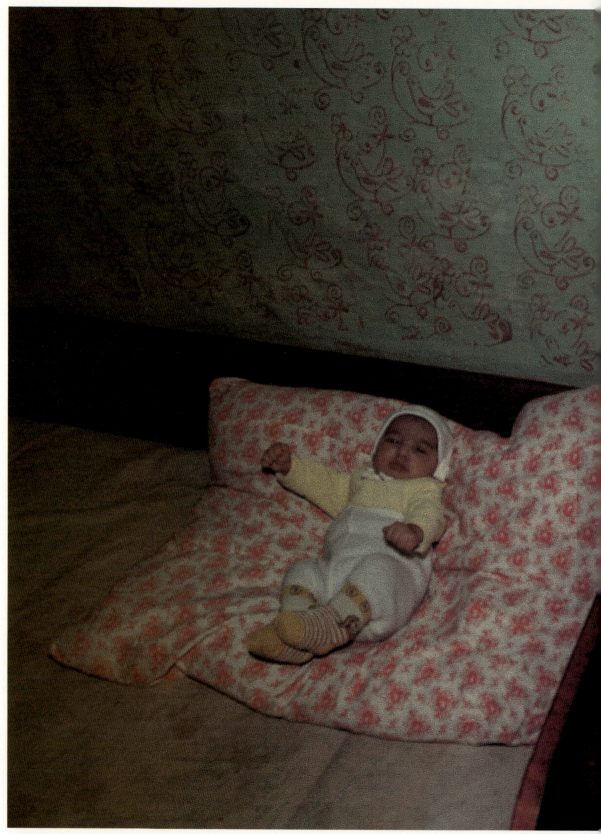

_ **SLOVAKIA** CHILD AT HOME IN A ROMA SETTLEMENT

_ **BURKINA FASO** CHILDREN AT HOME

_ FREIBURG **GERMANY** LOW-ENERGY APARTMENT COMPLEX

_ MISSISSIPPI **U.S.A.** HARRIS HOUSE BUILT FROM RECYCLED MATERIALS BY THE RURAL STUDIO

_ **MONGOLIA** TRADITIONAL FELT TENT

_ NEW DELHI **INDIA** INSIDE A QUARTER IN OLD DELHI

_ KYUSHU ISLAND **JAPAN** A ROOM

BAMBOO IS THE PLANET'S *fastest-growing* PLANT. IT CAN BE

HARVESTED IN 3 TO 5 YEARS; MOST SOFTWOODS REQUIRE 10 TO 20 YEARS.

Food

ALICE WATERS
CHEF AND OWNER OF CHEZ PANISSE RESTAURANT, U.S.A.

At the age of 19, I went eating in France. I tasted wonderful things. It was my first time for so many foods—and I liked everything. I will always remember one meal in particular; I've tried to describe it hundreds of times. It was at a small restaurant in a stone house in Brittany. The stairs led up to a dining room that seated no more than 12 at pink cloth-covered tables. Through the open windows you could see a garden and a stream that ran behind the house. The chef, a woman, announced the menu: cured ham and melon, trout with almonds, and a raspberry tart. The ham had been cured by a neighbor. The trout had been caught in the stream. The raspberries had been picked in the garden. This meal changed my life.

When I returned to California I wanted to open a restaurant that served meals like that one. Yet despite my enthusiasm, I soon found it wasn't easy to cook this way. What had made that meal in Brittany so extraordinary was the quality of its ingredients—they were local and absolutely fresh. Back home, the fish was frozen, the meat was full of hormones and antibiotics, and the vegetables had not only been shipped thousands of miles but had been bred to store well rather than taste good. The more I looked, the more clearly I could see that Americans were alienated from their food and disconnected from its sources. We had come

_ MARSEILLES **FRANCE** LOCAL SUPERMARKET

Food

ALICE WATERS
CHEF AND OWNER OF CHEZ PANISSE RESTAURANT, U.S.A.

At the age of 19, I went eating in France. I tasted wonderful things. It was my first time for so many foods—and I liked everything. I will always remember one meal in particular; I've tried to describe it hundreds of times. It was at a small restaurant in a stone house in Brittany. The stairs led up to a dining room that seated no more than 12 at pink cloth-covered tables. Through the open windows you could see a garden and a stream that ran behind the house. The chef, a woman, announced the menu: cured ham and melon, trout with almonds, and a raspberry tart. The ham had been cured by a neighbor. The trout had been caught in the stream. The raspberries had been picked in the garden. This meal changed my life.

When I returned to California I wanted to open a restaurant that served meals like that one. Yet despite my enthusiasm, I soon found it wasn't easy to cook this way. What had made that meal in Brittany so extraordinary was the quality of its ingredients—they were local and absolutely fresh. Back home, the fish was frozen, the meat was full of hormones and antibiotics, and the vegetables had not only been shipped thousands of miles but had been bred to store well rather than taste good. The more I looked, the more clearly I could see that Americans were alienated from their food and disconnected from its sources. We had come to devalue eating itself. Many people, even those I respected, simply didn't think that eating was important. Too often, food was described as mere fuel, an inconvenient necessity. The ritual of coming to the dinner table to share a wholesome, lovingly prepared meal was becoming an anachronism.

Yet not so long ago, the family meal was the primary reward—and the principal responsibility—of family living. The human behaviors we most prize can be learned, better than anywhere else, at the table. Families eating together cultivate courteousness, kindness, and generosity toward one another and toward strangers; and sharing and preparing food encourages appreciation and reverence for the bounty of nature.

By trivializing the essential act of eating, we not only fail to teach our children how to be human; we thoughtlessly support an industrialized network of food production that wreaks environmental havoc. By choosing mass-produced and fast food, we acquiesce to a network of food production that cuts every possible corner to increase profit. We support a kind of agriculture that wastes and poisons soil and water and subjects livestock to an unhealthful regime of drugs and unspeakably inhumane living conditions, and we favor a fishing industry that threatens entire species by scouring the oceans on a huge scale. When I started Chez Panisse, I came to realize that the everyday decisions we make about the food we eat are actually big decisions about the way we take care of the planet. I also found that if I wanted to cook the kind of food that I ate in France, I would have to start creating demand for the ingredients I wanted to use.

As word got out that my partners and I were particular about the food we wanted to serve, people started showing up at the kitchen door with food for sale. Neighbors with herb gardens would arrive with bouquets of fresh thyme and sorrel. A few eccentric enthusiasts would bring us baskets of wild chanterelles and morels. We found fishermen to deliver buckets of local Pacific mussels and fish that were caught by small boats off the California coast. In the summer, people would appear with wild blackberries; in the winter they brought lemons picked from neighbors' backyard trees. Over time we found farmers who grew delicious vegetables without pesticides or herbicides and ranchers who raised their animals conscientiously.

We discovered a pattern: the freshest, tastiest ingredients usually came from the most environmentally conscious producers. The organically grown apple, like the range-fed, drug-free steer, tastes best. There is a wonderful logic. By eating the best-tasting local food, we support the farmers, ranchers, and fishermen who take care of the planet. This is the lesson I have tried to pass on. Food is important. The decisions that we all make about the food we buy and the way we share it are among the most crucial of our lives. To bring about a humane, just, and sustainable future, we can start by buying from our local farmers' markets, cooking our food conscientiously, and eating with our families.

_ MARSEILLES **FRANCE** LOCAL SUPERMARKET

_ **GERMANY** PORK SAUSAGES FROM THE HERMANNSDORFER ORGANIC FARM

_ SOGUT **TURKEY** HOMEMADE BREADS AT A COUNTRY FAIR

_ **MALI** SAVE THE CHILDREN CREDIT SCHEME HELPS VILLAGES SET UP CEREAL BANKS

_ SOYAPANGO **EL SALVADOR** GIRL SEARCHES A CITY DUMP FOR DISCARDED BABY CHICKS FROM THE HATCHERY

THE NUMBER OF OVERFED PEOPLE IN THE WORLD NEARLY EQUALS THE NUMBER OF

UNDERFED PEOPLE: APPROXIMATELY 1.1 billion.

_ NAPLES **ITALY** LOCAL TRATTORIA CATERING TO A LUNCHTIME CROWD

_ NEW BRIGHTON **ENGLAND** CHIP SHOP AT SEASIDE RESORT

50 MILLION POUNDS OF

antibiotics ARE

PRODUCED IN THE U.S.A. EACH YEAR,

20 MILLION POUNDS OF WHICH ARE

ADMINISTERED TO LIVESTOCK.

_ MONOPOLI PUGLIA **ITALY** SEA URCHINS, A RAW FOOD DELICACY

_ BANUE **PHILIPPINES** PADDY FIELDS

_ **STRAIT OF GIBRALTAR** TUNA FISHERMEN AT SEA

_ RANGOON **MYANMAR** TYPICAL LOCAL RESTAURANT

Sustainable FARMING HAS GROWN INTO A

BUSINESS WORTH SOME $7.3 BILLION A YEAR IN THE EUROPEAN UNION

AND AROUND $15.6 BILLION WORLDWIDE.

_GALICIA **SPAIN** FARMER'S WIFE COLLECTING FRESH EGGS

_ **HUNGARY** HOMEMADE LOCAL SPECIALTIES BEING SOLD AT THE HUNGARIAN BORDER

_ NEAR GHAEMSHAHR **IRAN** RICE PLANTER'S MORNING MEAL

111

MCDONALD'S HAS **28,000** RESTAURANTS WORLDWIDE

AND OPENS APPROXIMATELY 2,000 NEW ONES EACH YEAR.

_ ALABAMA **U.S.A.** FAST-FOOD AND RELIGIOUS SIGNS ALONG A STATE HIGHWAY

_ NEAR GHAEMSHAHR **IRAN** RICE PLANTER'S MORNING MEAL

_ ONTARIO **CANADA** MENNONITE FARMERS HARVESTING FIELDS

_ **BURKINA FASO** YOUNG BOY WITH LOCALLY GROWN PRODUCE

MCDONALD'S HAS **28,000** RESTAURANTS WORLDWIDE

AND OPENS APPROXIMATELY 2,000 NEW ONES EACH YEAR.

_ ALABAMA **U.S.A.** FAST-FOOD AND RELIGIOUS SIGNS ALONG A STATE HIGHWAY

_ MADRID **SPAIN** EL MUSEO DEL JAMON (THE HAM MUSEUM)

_**BURKINA FASO** PIG GIVEN TO A RURAL FAMILY BY HEIFER INTERNATIONAL

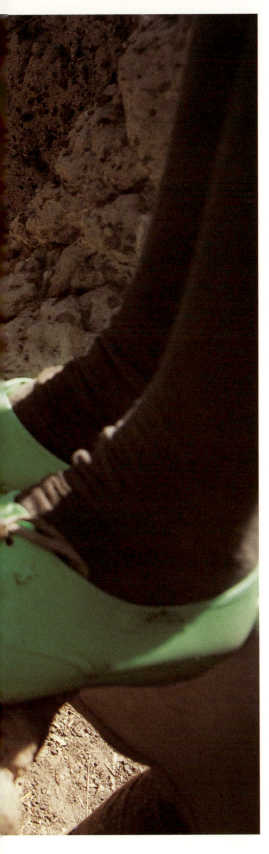

BETWEEN 1996 AND 2001, THE GLOBAL ACREAGE

FOR THREE MAJOR GENETICALLY ENGINEERED

crops—CORN, CANOLA, AND SOYBEANS—

GREW ABOUT 50-FOLD TO 113 MILLION ACRES.

Community

HER MAJESTY QUEEN NOOR OF JORDAN
CHAIR OF THE KING HUSSEIN FOUNDATION, JORDAN

Community is one of the most powerful forces in the history of humankind. It has shaped our nature as moral, social, and economic beings. Its scope extends from ancient hunter-gatherer clans to today's vast array of collaborative groups and ranges from vibrant village societies to charitable organizations and international-action associations. As communities, we come together to share experiences from feasts to funerals; we also work together to fight poverty, disease, environmental degradation, and other enduring scourges.

Community action has generally been a positive force in human society, but, as is true of all human structures, it has not always been benevolent. We can easily identify examples of communities that have been exclusive, hierarchical, intolerant, contemptuous, and violent. Horrifying bloodshed and the abandonment of humane values have occurred in the name of community. Borrowing language from basic arithmetic, we may need to distinguish between "lowest common denominator" communities, which can exalt inhumane values, and "highest common factor" communities, which strive to nurture and empower their members.

From my perspective, there are two fundamental values inherent in all benevolent communities: cooperation and the harnessing of that cooperation to achieve the material, societal, or spiritual good that individuals often cannot accomplish independently. The impetus to share rites of passage and common goals and ideals should be revered; this will aid us greatly as we face the challenges our species must meet as we move into the third millennium.

Much has been said and written over the past hundred years or so about the dangers of the loss of community, in the world's richest and poorest countries alike. Social analysts have warned that some of the economic and social advances of the late 19th and 20th centuries—from the emergence of dehumanized production systems to that of the global economy—may be sapping the values of community. Others feel that, because our nature is social, the concept of community will continue to thrive. From my own experience in working with local communities in Jordan, I agree with the latter. Community continues to thrive worldwide at what economists would call the micro and the macro levels.

The disciplines of anthropology, sociology, psychology, political science, and economics have taught us a lot about the dynamics of community at the micro, or local, level. Today, we have a better understanding than ever before of how local groups work. And there are remarkable examples from around the world of community adaptation and vitality—cases as diverse as poverty reduction in low-income countries or the creation of so-called enterprise zones in inner cities and depressed areas in some of the world's richest societies—which prove that the values of community are alive and well locally.

On an international level, the 20th century saw the evolution of peaceful, nonsectarian shared initiatives. These macro efforts were the first to reach beyond traditional military alliances or those of shared religious faith. Here I am referring to a variety of movements based on the concept of common action for the common good, including some with which I have been personally involved, such as the International Campaign to Ban Landmines. Other examples are the One World and Spaceship Earth movements, the concept—itself revolutionary—of global public goods, and the adherence of nations to the United Nations Millennium Development Goals.

My husband, King Hussein of Jordan, was a regional, national, and international leader whose goal was to promote collaborative leadership among, as well as within, communities. His vision was based on inclusiveness and mutual respect. This vision, sorely needed today, remains an inspiration to us all. Through the King Hussein Foundation, established in his memory and of which I am president, we are continuing his work. Our motto, "Building Bridges for Peace," reflects his commitment and his aims.

The King Hussein Foundation and its affiliates have worked for more than two decades to support projects that enable communities to implement their own social and economic advancement. Focusing on the principles of self-reliance and action, we have helped to empower approximately 70,000 people in village communities across Jordan to secure more fulfilling lives for themselves.

Community is an immensely powerful force. At best, it can help humanity to meet its noblest aspirations and satisfy its needs for tradition and ritual. In my mind it is intensely resilient, because it answers the human desire for shared values and common endeavor at all levels—local, national, and international. But it requires wise nurturing and leadership, so that its energy can work for the good in our increasingly interdependent world. Alone, we can often do little to better the lives of others; in community, we can rejoice together, provide solace for pain and loss, and use our common strength to better our world.

ACADEMIC achievement DROPS

SHARPLY FOR CHILDREN WHO WATCH MORE THAN 10 HOURS A WEEK OF TV.

_ BRASOV **ROMANIA** CHILDREN PLAYING

_ ULYANOVSK **RUSSIA** COOPERATIVE SUPPORT GROUP

_ KUALA LUMPUR **MALAYSIA** SUNWAY LAGOON WATERPARK AND CONDOS UNDER CONSTRUCTION

_ TOKYO **JAPAN** APARTMENT COMPLEX

PLEASE
NO FIREARMS
OR OTHER
WEAPONS
ALLOWED IN
BUILDING

_ NEW YORK CITY **U.S.A** ENTRANCE TO THE EMPIRE STATE BUILDING

_ ONTARIO **CANADA** SQUASH BEING HARVESTED

_ TAMPAKSIRING BALI **INDONESIA** "ODALAN" CELEBRATION RITUAL

_ ALI ABAD **IRAN** MOURNERS AT THE VILLAGE CEMETERY

_ SAMARKAND **UZBEKISTAN** WOMEN HAVING TEA AT THEIR LOCAL MARKET

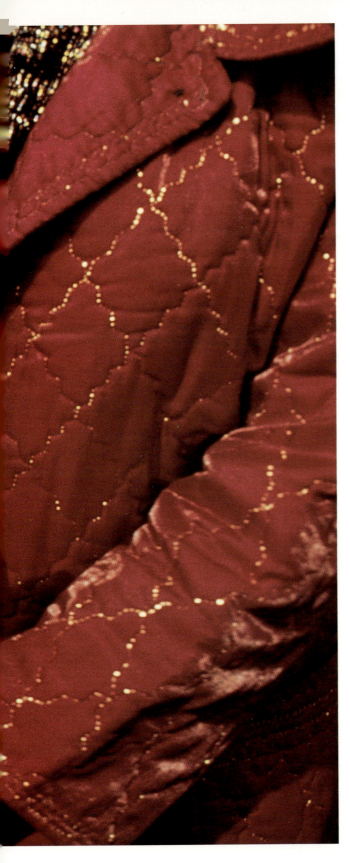

A TUPPERWARE DEMONSTRATION

STARTS EVERY 2 seconds

SOMEWHERE IN THE WORLD.

_ LONDON **ENGLAND** MULTIRACIAL CHILDREN PLAYING IN THE DOCKLANDS

_ PENWOOD FOREST **ENGLAND** NEWBERRY BYPASS DEMONSTRATION

_ KABUL **AFGHANISTAN** JADED MAIWAND, FORMERLY THE MAIN COMMERCIAL STREET

THERE ARE NEARLY 80 MILLION TEACHERS IN THE WORLD.

18 million MORE ARE NEEDED BY 2015.

_ ULYANOVSK **RUSSIA** KOLKHOZIEN MARKET

_ BENARES **INDIA** LIGHT CARRIERS AT A WEDDING

_ **MALI** MARKET IN DJENNE

_ **SINGAPORE** CHINESE FUNERAL BAND

_ MOSCOW **RUSSIA** SQUATTERS, COMMUNITY FOR ARTISTS

_ **MALI** CHILDREN IN THEIR CLASSROOM

_ JHANSI **INDIA** DEVELOPMENT ALTERNATIVES ECO-PAPER FACTORY

_ ALABAMA **U.S.A** COMMUNITY CENTER MADE WITH SALVAGED MATERIALS

_ **HONG KONG** SHANGHAI BANKING CORPORATION OFFICE BUILDING

_ **RWANDA** MGWANZA REFUGEE CAMP

HALF OF THE $6{,}800$ LANGUAGES

SPOKEN TODAY ARE EXPECTED TO BECOME

EXTINCT BY THE END OF THIS CENTURY.

_ AJIEP **SUDAN** WORLD FOOD PROGRAMME DISTRIBUTION POINT

_ **RWANDA** MGWANZA REFUGEE CAMP

HALF OF THE $6,800$ LANGUAGES

SPOKEN TODAY ARE EXPECTED TO BECOME

EXTINCT BY THE END OF THIS CENTURY.

Tragedy

HIS HOLINESS THE DALAI LAMA
SPIRITUAL AND TEMPORAL LEADER OF THE TIBETAN PEOPLE

Tragedy invariably entails loss – loss of life, of family and friends, of land, of home, of health or of freedom. The images in this section of this book portray tragedy and loss that have arisen as a result of natural disasters, the nuclear accident at Chernobyl, war, and terrorist attack.

Many of the world's problems and conflicts arise because we have lost sight of the basic humanity that binds us all together as a human family. We tend to forget that despite the diversity of race, religion, ideology and so forth, people are equal in their basic wish for peace and happiness.

Although war has always been part of human history, in ancient times there were winners and losers. If another global conflict were to occur now, there would be no winners at all. Realizing this danger, steps are being taken to eliminate weapons of mass destruction. Nonetheless, in a volatile world, the risk remains as long as even a handful of these weapons continue to exist.

If we look back at the development of the 20th century, the most devastating cause of human suffering, of deprivation of human dignity, freedom and peace has been the culture of violence in resolving differences and conflicts. In some ways, the 20th century can be called the century of war and bloodshed. The challenge before us, therefore, is to make this century a century of dialogue and of peaceful co-existence.

Similarly, the problems of poverty, overpopulation, and destruction of the environment that face the global community today are problems that we have to address together. No single community or nation can expect to solve them on its own. In ancient times, each village was more or less self-sufficient and independent. There was neither the need nor the expectation of cooperation with others outside the village. You survived by doing everything yourself. The situation now has completely changed. It has become very old-fashioned to think only in terms of my nation or my country, let alone my village. Therefore, I repeat that universal responsibility is the real key to overcoming our problems.

My personal understanding of tragedy is that of one in exile. The tragedy of my land and my people is their loss of liberty. All human beings yearn for freedom, equality, and dignity, and we all have a right to achieve them. Yet Tibetans are among those oppressed peoples who have been denied the opportunity to express and implement their right to self-determination.

When Tibet was still free, we cultivated our natural isolation, mistakenly thinking that we could prolong our peace and security that way. Consequently, we paid little attention to the changes taking place in the world outside. Later, we learned the hard way that in the international arena, awareness and relationships with other countries were of utmost importance.

In human societies there will always be differences of views and interests. But the reality today is that we are all inter-dependent and have to co-exist on this small planet. Therefore, the only sensible and intelligent way of resolving differences and clashes of interests, whether between individuals or nations, is through dialogue. The promotion of a culture of dialogue and non-violence for the future of mankind is thus an important task for the international community. It is not enough for governments to endorse the principle of non-violence or hold it high without any appropriate action to promote it.

It is also natural that we should face obstacles in pursuit of our goals. But if we remain passive, making no effort to solve the problems we meet, conflicts will arise and hindrances will grow. Transforming these obstacles into opportunities for positive growth is a challenge to our human ingenuity. To achieve this requires patience, compassion and the use of our intelligence.

AT THE END OF 2001,

AN ESTIMATED 40 MILLION PEOPLE WORLDWIDE

WERE LIVING WITH HIV, APPROXIMATELY

ONE-THIRD OF WHOM WERE BETWEEN THE

AGES OF 15 AND 24. MOST OF THEM

DID NOT KNOW THEY WERE CARRYING

THE virus.

_ MANAUS **BRAZIL** FLOODING ON THE OUTSKIRTS OF THE CITY

_ AJIEP **SUDAN** WORLD FOOD PROGRAMME DISTRIBUTION POINT

_ GROZNY **RUSSIA** LAST ITEM ON THE STALL BEFORE THE MARKET CLOSES FOR CURFEW

155

_ JERUSALEM **ISRAEL** DEMONSTRATOR AT THE WAILING WALL

_ TAICHUNG **TAIWAN** EARTHQUAKE DAMAGE

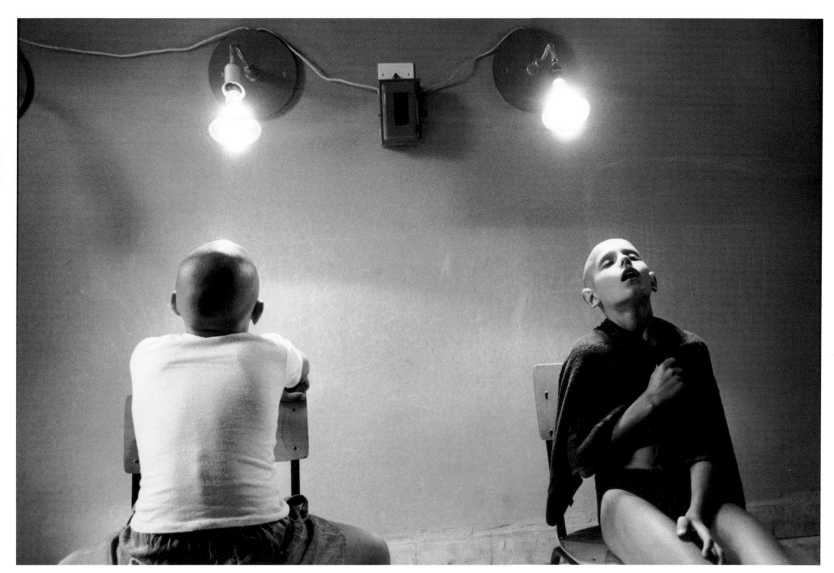

_ TARARA **CUBA** VICTIMS OF THE SOVIET CHERNOBYL NUCLEAR CATASTROPHE LIVING IN CUBA

NEARLY 2 MILLION CHILDREN DIE EVERY YEAR FROM DIARRHEAL DISEASES CAUSED BY

contaminated WATER AND FOOD, AND POOR HYGIENE.

_ LONDON **ENGLAND** LORA TAKES HEROIN WHILE HER DAUGHTER WATCHES TELEVISION

_ OGADEN **ETHIOPIA** DISPLAY OF DEAD CATTLE DRAWS ATTENTION TO A HUMANITARIAN CRISIS

_ **GAZA STRIP** PALESTINIAN MOTHER HOLDING A PHOTO OF HER DECEASED SON

_ BRANDENBURG **GERMANY** OPEN-CAST MINE

_ **HONG KONG** VIETNAMESE CHILD DRINKS WATER AT A REFUGEE CAMP

_ **SOMALIA** ARMED TRUCK PASSES HUMAN REMAINS

IN A WORLD WHERE FOOD SUPPLIES ARE PLENTIFUL, ALMOST 800 MILLION PEOPLE

IN THE DEVELOPING WORLD ARE CHRONICALLY hungry.

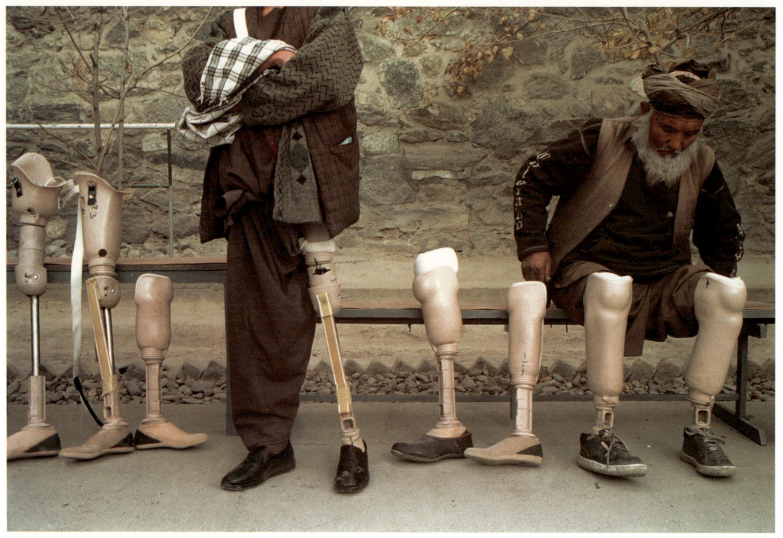

_ KABUL **AFGHANISTAN** MEN WOUNDED BY LAND MINES

THERE ARE 22 MILLION REFUGEES, ASYLUM SEEKERS,

AND INTERNALLY DISPLACED PERSONS IN THE WORLD,

ACCOUNTING FOR APPROXIMATELY ONE OUT OF EVERY

275 people ON EARTH.

_ NEW YORK CITY **U.S.A.** SEPTEMBER 11, 2001, VIEW OF THE DISASTER FROM BROOKLYN

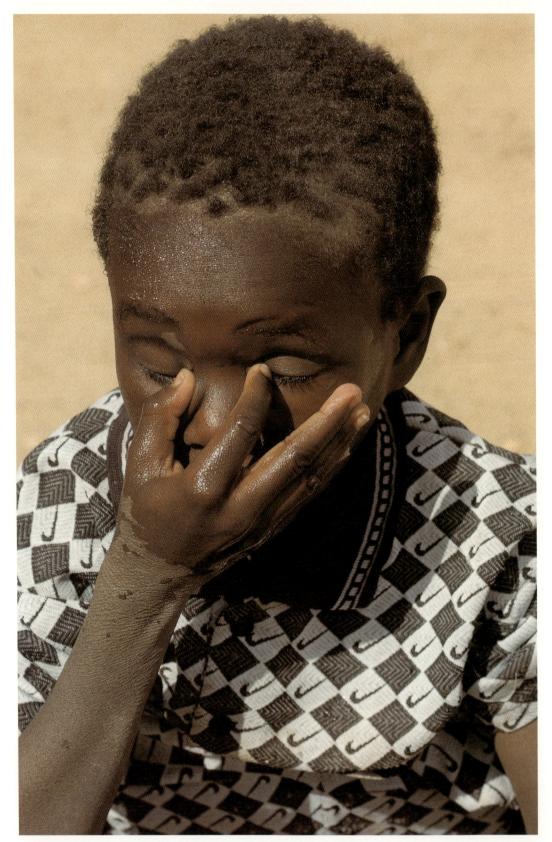

_ **BURKINA FASO** BLIND CHILD AT A SCHOOL RUN BY HELEN KELLER WORLDWIDE

_ LONDON **ENGLAND** POVERTY-STRICKEN HOME IN WHITECHAPEL

THE ILLEGAL BUSINESS OF migrant SMUGGLING NETS $7 BILLION ANNUALLY.

_ BUCHAREST **ROMANIA** HOMELESS PEOPLE EAT NEAR A FOOD DISTRIBUTION CENTER

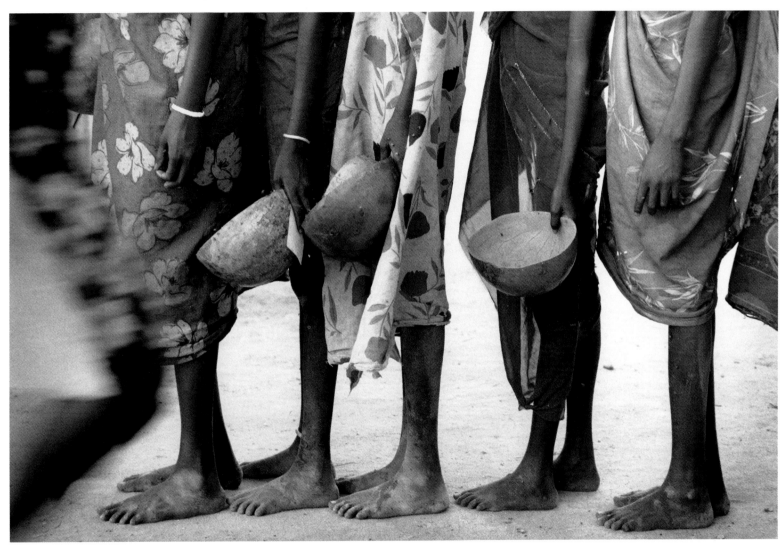

_ LEER **SUDAN** FOOD QUEUE AT THE HOSPITAL

IN 1960, THE ARAL SEA WAS THE WORLD'S FOURTH-LARGEST LAKE, AT 26,250 SQUARE MILES. BY 2001, ITS VOLUME HAD *decreased* BY 75% BECAUSE OF MISMANAGED IRRIGATION PRACTICES.

_ MUYNAK **UZBEKISTAN** ABANDONED SHIPS AT THE EDGE OF WHAT WAS THE ARAL SEA

_ KUKES **ALBANIA** NEW ARRIVALS AWAIT ADMITTANCE TO REFUGEE CAMPS

Pleasure

PETER A. SELIGMANN
CHAIRMAN AND C.E.O. OF CONSERVATION INTERNATIONAL, U.S.A.

Approach a magnificent waterfall or hear a lion roar in the wild, and your heart beats a little faster. Recline in the soothing warmth of a natural hot spring, and you feel a sense of serenity. Kick a soccer ball with your friends, and you engage in pure delight. These are just some of the infinite pleasures enjoyed by people throughout the world.

While we often find simple pleasures close to home, time and again most of us are struck by wanderlust, for we know that travel opens new dimensions to our lives and souls. This hunger to explore beyond the immediate borders of our everyday life motivates what is arguably the world's largest business: tourism. The human passion for traveling generates an estimated U.S. $3 trillion in annual revenues. The World Tourism Organization predicts that by the year 2010 the industry will have grown fourfold from its 1996 level.

Nature-based tourism has become one of the fastest-growing sectors within the industry, increasing at an annual rate of between 10 and 30 percent a year. In our hectic, high-tech, traffic-snarled world, it is no surprise that people seek sanctuary in natural places. Via the internet or television, we can see just about anything—from the inside of a space station orbiting Earth to the subterranean tunnels of ants in the Amazon. But experiencing nature firsthand provides spiritual and physical rejuvenation. Nothing can replace the living, natural world.

The upward trend in nature tourism—wildlife safaris, wilderness trekking, river rafting—both threatens fragile ecosystems and local populations and provides opportunities for sustainable development. But nature tourism and ecotourism, often confused, are not the same. Ecotourism is responsible travel that conserves nature and sustains the well-being of local peoples. At Conservation International, our Ecotourism Department works actively with local communities, government agencies, and private-sector partners to promote responsible travel around the world. We believe that tourism can be a major factor in the preservation of nature's ecosystems and that even large-scale tourism companies can integrate conservation into their day-to-day operations. In developing tourism, we can get it right and provide stable, local economic benefits while protecting ecosystems, or we can get it terribly wrong and destroy natural places while offering little improvement to local people's lives.

A stark example of tourism development gone awry took place along Mexico's eastern coast in the 1970s. Prior to development, only 12 families lived on the barrier island of Cancún. The entire area was made up of relatively untouched rain forests and pristine beaches and was inhabited by an indigenous Maya population of about 45,000. Today, Cancún, whose permanent population is approximately 300,000, receives more than 2.6 million visitors a year and maintains over 20,000 hotel rooms.

Environmental and social impacts were given secondary importance in Cancún's development plan. For instance, no provisions were made for housing migrants who work and live in the area. As a result, a shantytown developed, in which the sewage of 75 percent of the population is untreated. The mangrove and inland forests were cut down, swamps and lagoons were filled, and dunes were removed. Many bird, marine, and other animal species vanished.

On the opposite end of the spectrum is Chalalan Ecolodge in Bolivia's Madidi National Park. Chalalan is the result of a partnership between the rain-forest community of San José Uchupiamonas and Conservation International, with support from the InterAmerican Development Bank. The goal was to provide a viable ecotourism business wholly owned by the local people while promoting biodiversity conservation. Chalalan today offers an economic alternative to destructive logging. Villagers have learned all aspects of running a lodge, from marketing and management to housekeeping and food preparation. In 2001 the community assumed full ownership and management of the lodge, and today 60 families receive economic benefits. Visitors regularly spot monkeys, tapir, capybaras, alligators, and wild pigs, as well as some 340 bird species.

While Chalalan illustrates how a small community can benefit from ecotourism, the appeal of responsible planning and development is becoming more obvious to the larger tourism industry as well. After all, if the industry fails to protect natural and cultural heritage, it will be spoiling the very attractions it depends on for success.

In today's tumultuous world, ecotourism's fundamental principles of involving the local community, respecting local cultures, and protecting nature can serve as a powerful salve for global tensions. As more and more people explore and enjoy the wonders of nature and benefit from the many pleasures travel provides, I believe that we human beings will ultimately find a way to live in harmony with our natural world. If we can accomplish that, then there is hope that we can also live in harmony with one another.

"GROSS NATIONAL happiness IS MORE IMPORTANT THAN GROSS NATIONAL PRODUCT."

_ THE KING OF BHUTAN.

_ BENTOTA **SRI LANKA** TOURISM IN SRI LANKA

_ SÃO PAULO **BRAZIL** SOCCER IN THE STREETS OF THE FAVELA HELIOPOLIS

_ OAXACA **MEXICO** WOMEN DANCING DURING AN ANNUAL FESTIVAL

_ NEW YORK CITY **U.S.A.** SUNBATHING IN CENTRAL PARK

_ GALÁPAGOS ISLANDS **ECUADOR** TOURISTS ARRIVING IN BALTRA

50 million PEOPLE PLAY GOLF WORLDWIDE. EACH YEAR,

LAND SURFACE EQUIVALENT TO THE SIZE OF PARIS IS CLEARED FOR GOLF COURSES.

_ **ZIMBABWE** ROYAL HARARE GOLF CLUB

_ MASSAOUA **ERITREA** POOL

_ KAWAYU **JAPAN** RELAXING IN A NATURAL HOT SPRING

_ COTE D'AZUR **FRANCE** SUNBATHING AT THE BEACH

_ NEW MEXICO **U.S.A.** VISITORS AT THE SITE OF THE FIRST ATOMIC BOMB EXPLOSION

_ MILAN **ITALY** CYCLISTS

_ QUARTZSITE ARIZONA **U.S.A.** TRAILER PARK FOR WINTER VACATIONERS IN THE ARIZONA DESERT

77% OF THE 7 BILLION KG OF TRASH DUMPED INTO

THE OCEAN EACH YEAR COMES FROM CRUISE SHIPS.

_ LAS VEGAS NEVADA **U.S.A.** NEW YORK HOTEL ON "THE STRIP"

_ QUARTZSITE ARIZONA **U.S.A.** TRAILER PARK FOR WINTER VACATIONERS IN THE ARIZONA DESERT

77% OF THE 7 BILLION KG OF TRASH DUMPED INTO

THE OCEAN EACH YEAR COMES FROM CRUISE SHIPS.

_ GALÁPAGOS ISLANDS **ECUADOR** FISHING AND TOURIST BOATS IN PUERTA AYORA

FOOTBALL, COMMONLY KNOWN AS SOCCER IN THE

UNITED STATES, IS THE number one

SPORT AROUND THE WORLD, WITH MORE THAN 240 MILLION

ACTIVE FOOTBALLERS AND 5 MILLION

REFEREES AND OFFICIALS.

_ LAS VEGAS NEVADA **U.S.A.** NEW YORK HOTEL ON "THE STRIP"

_ WEST BANK GAZA **ISRAEL** CHILDREN IN THE ONLY POOLROOM IN THE GAZA STRIP

_ MONTANA **U.S.A.** SWIFTCURRENT LAKE, GLACIER NATIONAL PARK

_ CHOLUTECA **HONDURAS** CHILDREN PLAYING BASKETBALL IN A SCHOOL FOR DISPLACED FAMILIES

IN THE GALÁPAGOS ISLANDS, TOURISM

GENERATES $2,000,000

A YEAR FOR THE GALÁPAGOS NATIONAL PARK,

MORE THAN DOUBLE THE PARK'S FUNDING FROM

THE GOVERNMENT OF ECUADOR.

_ RIO DE JANEIRO **BRAZIL** FAVELLA BALLERINAS

_ **CANARY ISLANDS** TOURIST ON A CAMEL TREK ACROSS AN OLD VOLCANO

_ HAVANA **CUBA** MEN PLAYING DOMINOES

Economy

JOHN ELKINGTON
CHAIR OF SUSTAINABILITY, U.K.

"It's the economy, stupid!" may once have been a resonant political catchphrase, but in the wake of the avalanche-like collapse of much of the new economy, followed by the teeth-rattling aftershocks from the failure of Enron, should we now talk in terms of "the stupid economy"? Tempting, but the answer is no. It may be messy, but this is how economies learn.

That said, the scale of the lessons that political and business leaders must now absorb is almost unparalleled. Early in 2002, for example, the World Economic Forum (WEF) opened its doors in New York. The event saw the global élite struggling to understand and respond to a new agenda fueled by concerns about terrorism, militant Islam, antiglobalization, recession, and the "dot-bomb" phenomenon.

Those organizing the forum had learned from earlier reverses, including protests the previous year in their homeland, Switzerland. So the 2002 WEF process was more transparent, with considerably greater "civil society" participation. The demonstrators outside kept up a constant drumbeat of protest, but dissent had begun to come in from the cold. The new agenda was forcefully articulated not just by the likes of rock singer Bono of U2 or Archbishop Desmond Tutu but also by the chief executives of companies such as AOL Time Warner, Cisco Systems, Microsoft, and Shell—and in language that a few years ago would have been used only by campaigners. It was a question not so much of what was being said but by whom.

All this represents one more symptom of the gathering third wave of societal pressure on rich-world economies. The first wave built steadily from 1960, peaking between 1969 and 1973. The first great downwave followed, running from 1974 to 1987. Through the mid-1970s, a secondary wave of environmental legislation swept across the industrialized world. Industry went into compliance mode. Acid rain had a major impact on EU politics in the early 1980s, but this was a period of conservative politics, with energetic attempts to roll back environmental legislation. A major turning point came in 1987, however, with the publication of *Our Common Future* by the Brundtland Commission, which introduced the term "sustainable development" into the political mainstream.

The second wave began in 1988. Issues like ozone depletion and rain-forest destruction helped fuel a new movement: green consumerism. The peak of the second wave ran from 1988 to 1991. The second downwave followed in 1991 and lasted through much of the following decade. The 1992 UN Earth Summit in Rio delayed the impending downwave, triggering spikes in media coverage of issues like climate change and biodiversity, but against a falling trend in public interest. There would be further spikes, too, driven by controversies around companies like Shell, Monsanto, and Nike and by public concerns—at least in Europe—about mad cow disease and genetically modified foods.

The third wave began in 1999. The so-called Battle of Seattle saw environmental, labor, and social activists challenging the World Trade Organization (WTO). The big media story was the antiglobalization (or at least anti-corporate-globalization) movement. High-profile protests against the World Bank, the G8, WEF, and other institutions helped push global governance issues up the political priorities list.

Our forecast as 2002 dawned was that the third, "globalization" wave would continue to develop for 12 to 18 months, with the 2002 UN World Summit on Sustainable Development (WSSD) helping keep the agenda on the boil. Farther afield, we can expect fourth and fifth waves, very likely on shorter time frequencies and—possibly—with fewer dramatic fluctuations in public interest.

As these waves and downwaves develop, expect to see "the Chrysalis Economy" evolve. This will be an era of intense economic metamorphosis. Ours is a "Caterpillar Economy," often highly destructive of natural, social, and other forms of capital. Although we have tinkered with our technologies, business models, and value webs for decades, hoping to achieve anything between 5 percent and Factor 2 (50 percent) improvements in their eco-efficiency, the 21st century's demographic and lifestyle trends will demand Factor 4 (75 percent), Factor 10 (90 percent), and even higher levels of improvement. We will need to innovate both at the level of the function (that is, not just a better car, but better mobility or access solutions) and at the level of the total system (that is, how we design cities and, for example, control urban sprawl).

The events of September 11, 2001, served notice that both absolute poverty and relative poverty will be major political issues in the future. Either we satisfy the needs of some 10 billion people in ways that protect—and ultimately regenerate—Earth's natural capital, or the 21st century could be even bloodier than the 20th.

_ ORLANDO **FLORIDA** VISITOR READY TO CONQUER DISNEYLAND

_ ZURICH **SWITZERLAND** PIGGY BANK

IN SENEGAL, AS MUCH AS 80% OF A HOUSEHOLD BUDGET

COMES FROM REMITTANCES, THE EARNINGS THAT MIGRANT WORKERS SEND

BACK HOME. THESE REMITTANCES ARE BECOMING AN

INCREASINGLY IMPORTANT PART OF THE economies

OF DEVELOPING NATIONS.

_ GIZA **EGYPT** SOUVENIR SELLER AT THE PYRAMIDS

_ HONG KONG **CHINA** HONG KONG STOCK EXCHANGE

_ CHICAGO ILLINOIS **U.S.A.** CHICAGO BOARD OF TRADE

_ PARIS **FRANCE** WHOLESALE SUPERMARKET

_ SHANGHAI **CHINA** ONE OF THE MANY STOCK EXCHANGE OFFICES

IN 2001,  WAS INVESTED

IN SOCIALLY RESPONSIBLE MUTUAL FUNDS.

_ ULSAN **SOUTH KOREA** ONE OF THE MAIN AUTO PLANTS OF HYUNDAI MOTORS

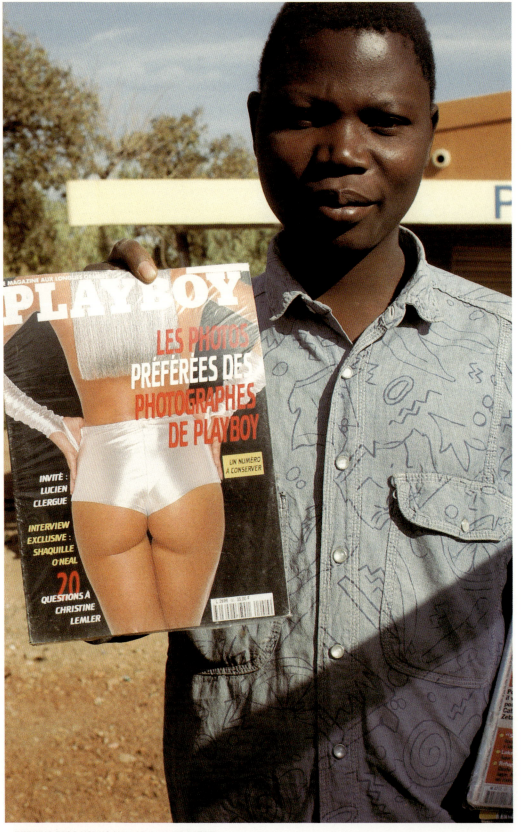

_ **BURKINA FASO** YOUNG MAN SELLING MAGAZINE

_ **MALI** TRANSPORTATION OF GOODS

_ LOS ANGELES **CALIFORNIA** TEAM OF CATERERS FOR A CHARITY FUNCTION

_ WUHAN **CHINA** FARMER WORKING NEAR WUHAN IRON & STEEL COMPANY

The gap BETWEEN THE RICH AND THE POOR IS WIDENING: IN 1970, THE RICHEST

10% OF THE WORLD'S POPULATION WERE 30 TIMES RICHER THAN THE 10% POOREST;

TODAY THEY ARE 74 TIMES RICHER.

TRENDS IN THE SUSTAINABLE

BUSINESS MARKETPLACE IN 2001 INCLUDED

A 38% growth IN U.S. ORGANIC

FOODS SALES, A 20% GROWTH

IN THE WIND POWER INDUSTRY, AND A

25% GROWTH IN SOLAR ENERGY.

_ KOSOVO **YUGOSLAVIA** ETHNIC ALBANIANS COLLECTING VALUABLE GOODS IN A GARBAGE DUMP

_ NEW YORK CITY **U.S.A.** VESUVIO BAKERY IN SOHO

_ KOWLOON **HONG KONG** WOMEN'S CLOTHING SALE

IN 2001, THERE WERE SOME 520 MILLION *internet* USERS AND

NEARLY 1 BILLION CELLULAR PHONE SUBSCRIBERS IN THE WORLD.

_ CUBATAO **BRAZIL** INDUSTRIAL COMPLEX PRODUCING CEMENT IN A HEAVILY POLLUTED TOWN

_ ISTANBUL **TURKEY**·STREET VENDOR

_ **SENEGAL** UNDP SOAP PROJECT FOSTERING ECONOMIC DEVELOPMENT

SALES OF BLOCKBUSTER drugs

LIKE VIAGRA®, WHICH TOTALED $1.5 BILLION IN 2001,

EXCEED THE ENTIRE HEALTH BUDGETS—

NOT TO MENTION THE MEDICINE BUDGETS—

OF MOST DEVELOPING NATIONS.

_ CALIFORNIA **U.S.A.** DOMINUS WINERY'S GABION WALL THAT REDUCES ENERGY CONSUMPTION

_ LONDON **ENGLAND** COMMUTERS GOING TO WORK ACROSS LONDON BRIDGE

Progress

MAURICE STRONG
SPECIAL ADVISOR TO THE SECRETARY-GENERAL OF
THE UNITED NATIONS, CANADA

Since the first global conference on the environment, held in Stockholm, Sweden, in 1972, and the Earth Summit in Rio de Janeiro in 1992, it is important that we reflect on the lessons of the past 30 years and the prospects for the future. During the past three decades we have made notable progress in defining the formidable nature of the challenges we face if the human community is to achieve the secure, sustainable, and equitable future to which all people aspire. It is a future that I am convinced is achievable, but only if in the first period of this new millennium we make the fundamental "change of course" called for by business leaders at the Earth Summit at Rio de Janeiro in 1992.

We have still not made that change of course and will not do so unless we take the decisions and actions that will break the inertia that continues to propel us along a course that is not sustainable. As an optimist, I continue to believe that such a change of course is possible. But as a realist, I am deeply concerned that, despite all the knowledge we have gained and the progress we have made since Stockholm first put the issue on the international agenda, we have still not demonstrated the degree of political will or the sense of priorities that such a change of course requires.

The events of September 11 have dramatically brought home to us that the phenomenon we now refer to as globalization, which has opened up so many new and exciting opportunities, has also united us in facing a new generation of risks and vulnerabilities: risks to our personal security and the security of our homes, offices, and communities as well as to the security of Earth's life-support systems, on which the survival and well-being of the entire human family depend. These risks and vulnerabilities are inextricably linked through the complex, systemic processes of globalization by which human activities are shaping the human future. They cannot be understood or dealt with in isolation. Nor can they be managed alone by any nation, however powerful. Indeed, they require a degree of cooperation beyond anything we seem yet prepared to accept.

Certainly, there have been many success stories, which demonstrate that it is possible to bring our economic life into a positive balance with our environmental and social systems by making the transition to a sustainable development pathway. For instance, there are more consumer ecoproducts than ever, ranging from clothing to kitchenware, electronics, furniture, and cars; chlorofluorocarbon emissions have been significantly reduced; the use of alternative energies is on the rise; and some 200 international environmental agreements have been signed to date.

On a global basis, we have the knowledge, the resources, and the capacities to build in this new millennium a civilization and mode of life in which pollution and poverty are eradicated; to see to it that the benefits that knowledge and technology afford be made available universally; and to ensure all inhabitants of Earth access to a better life and a secure, sustainable future, which is clearly within our reach.

Ours is the wealthiest civilization ever. We have yet to demonstrate that it is the wisest.

I am persuaded that the 21st century will be decisive for the human species, for we are now in a very real sense the trustees of our own future. The direction of the human future will be largely set in the first decades of this century. All the evidence of environmental degradation, social tension, and intercommunal conflict we have seen to date have occurred at levels of population and human activity that are a great deal lower than they will be in the period ahead. As we move into the 21st century, the risks we face from the mounting dangers to the environment, resource base, and life-support systems on which all life on Earth depends are far greater than the risks we face or have faced in our conflicts with one another.

A new paradigm of cooperative global governance is the only feasible basis on which we can manage these risks and realize the immense potential for progress and fulfillment for the entire human family that is within our reach. In our attempts to do this we are locked in a struggle between the world's ecosystems and its ego systems. It is the ego systems—the nations, the institutions, and, indeed, the individuals—that will have to change and that are so resistant to change. This will take a major shift in the current political mind-set. Necessity will compel such a shift eventually. The question is: Can we really afford the costs and the risks of waiting?

_ **HONG KONG** CONSTRUCTION OF THE TSING MAI BRIDGE

IN THE NETHERLANDS, OZONE-DEPLETING SUBSTANCES HAVE BEEN PHASED OUT,

WASTE DISPOSAL REDUCED BY 60%, recycling INCREASED TO 70%,

AND SULFUR DIOXIDE EMISSIONS FROM POWER PLANTS DECREASED BY 70%.

_ SEINE-MARITIME **FRANCE** EIGHTY TRUCKS ON THE PONT DE NORMANDIE FOR WEIGHT TESTS

_ LONDON **ENGLAND** LLOYD'S BUILDING

_ SEINE-MARITIME **FRANCE** EIGHTY TRUCKS ON THE PONT DE NORMANDIE FOR WEIGHT TESTS

_ CALIFORNIA **U.S.A.** FUTURISTIC ARCHITECTURE

_ ALMERIA **SPAIN** ALMERIA SOLAR PLATFORM, AN EXPERIMENTAL SOLAR INSTALLATION

_ LONDON **ENGLAND** LLOYD'S BUILDING

_ KERALA **INDIA** PREPARING COCONUT OIL

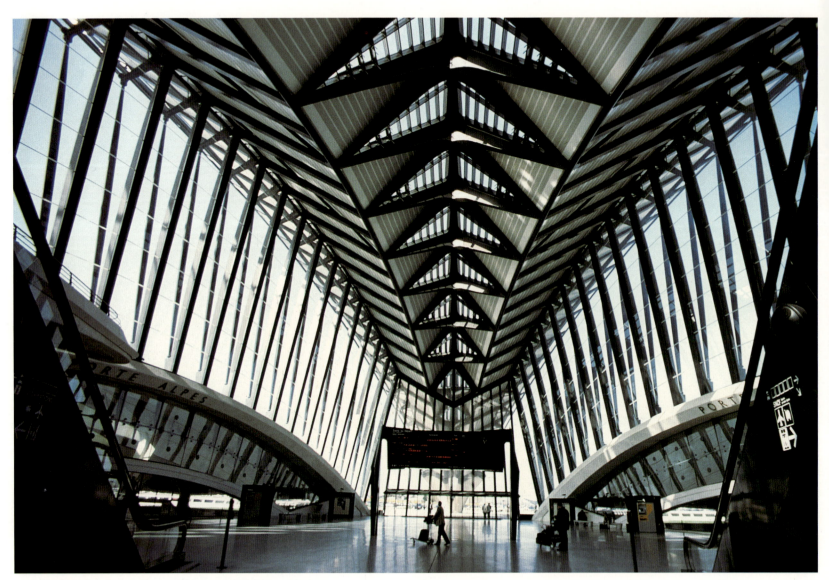

_ LYON **FRANCE** TGV TRAIN STATION AT SATOLAS AIRPORT

_ CORNWALL **ENGLAND** GIANT PUFFBALLS OF THE TROPICS BIOME

THE recycling OF PAPER

REDUCES AIR POLLUTION BY ABOUT 75%.

SUBSTITUTING STEEL SCRAP FOR VIRGIN ORE

LOWERS AIR EMISSIONS BY 85% AND WATER

POLLUTION BY 76%.

_ JINSHANLING **CHINA** INSTALLATION OF 1000 SCULPTURES, MADE OF GARBAGE, ON THE GREAT WALL

_ TOKYO **JAPAN** JR STATION MORNING RUSH HOUR

_ **SLOVAKIA** ROMA PEOPLE'S HOME WITH A SATELLITE DISH

_ CORNWALL **ENGLAND** DELABOLE WIND FARMS

THE FASTEST-GROWING

ENERGY SECTOR IS

wind power,

WHICH IN 2001 GENERATED AN

ESTIMATED $7 BILLION

IN BUSINESS.

_ **BOLIVIA** URBAN SCENERY

_ FREIBURG **GERMANY** URBAN COMMUNITY BUILT ACCORDING TO ECOLOGICAL CONSIDERATIONS

_ **THE NETHERLANDS** DUTCH BIKE ROUTE

_ LOFOTEN ISLANDS **NORWAY** SALMON FARM

_ ALABAMA **U.S.A.** YANCEY CHAPEL, BUILT USING RECYCLED TIRES AND OTHER SALVAGED MATERIALS

_ SANTIAGO **CHILE** MANUFACTURING HOME INDUSTRY FINANCED BY A BANK FOR THE POOR PROJECT

_ BERLIN **GERMANY** NORMAN FOSTER DOME ON THE TOP OF THE REICHSTAG

_ **THAILAND** POPULATION AND COMMUNITY DEVELOPMENT PROJECT

_ BRITTANY **FRANCE** TREATMENT CENTER FOR BIRDS

_ CHIBA **JAPAN** ORGANIC AGRICULTURAL PROJECT BY OISCA

BICYCLING LOWERS CARBON DIOXIDE POLLUTION, REDUCES OBESITY, INCREASES PHYSICAL FITNESS, AND alleviates CONGESTION.

CONTRIBUTORS

BEATRICE BIIRA, UGANDA
Beatrice Biira is an 18-year-old Ugandan woman whose life story was told in *Beatrice's Goat,* a *New York Times* children's picture books best-seller. Beatrice lived in poverty during her childhood until Heifer International gave her family a goat and, thanks to the income generated, turned her dream of attending school into reality. She will attend college in the U.S.A. on a full scholarship.

HIS HOLINESS THE DALAI LAMA, TIBET
H.H. Tenzin Gyatso, the 14th Dalai Lama, is the spiritual and temporal leader of the Tibetan people. He has been internationally acclaimed for his steadfast dedication to peace and non-violence and their propagation for resolving international conflicts, human rights issues, and global environmental problems. In 1989 he was awarded the Nobel Peace Prize. The Dalai Lama is also well known for his promotion of interreligious harmony and basic human values.

NITIN DESAI, INDIA
Nitin Desai is under-secretary-general for the Department of Economic and Social Affairs at the United Nations and secretary-general of the World Summit on Sustainable Development. He has been a member of the Commonwealth Secretariat Expert Group on Climate Change and has published several articles and papers on development planning, regional economics, industry, energy and international economic relations.

JOHN ELKINGTON, U.K.
John Elkington is chair of SustainAbility, based in London and New York, and author of 17 books, most recently *The Chrysalis Economy: How Citizen CEOs and Corporations Can Fuse Values and Value Creation* (John Wiley, 2001). In 1989 he was elected to the UN Global 500 Roll of Honor for his "outstanding environmental achievements."

LESLIE HOFFMAN, U.S.A.
Leslie Hoffman has been the executive director at the Earth Pledge Foundation since 1994. She has led Earth Pledge in several publishing efforts, including the *Sustainable Cities, Sustainable Cuisine,* and *Sustainable Architecture White Papers* series. Hoffman employed her architecture and construction background in the development of Earth Pledge's office, a renovation of a New York City townhouse, which includes a green roof system and an array of eco-sensitive building and design products.

DR. THOMAS E. LOVEJOY, U.S.A.
Dr. Thomas E. Lovejoy is president of The H. John Heinz III Center for Science, Economics and the Environment and research associate at the Smithsonian Institution in Washington, D.C. He is also founder of the public television series *Nature*; specialist in environmental biology of the tropics and Latin America; and co-editor of *Global Warming and Biological Diversity* (Yale University Press, 1992).

HER MAJESTY QUEEN NOOR, JORDAN
Her Majesty Queen Noor is Chair of the King Hussein Foundation and President of the United World Colleges. Queen Noor is Chair of the U.N. University Leadership Academy, Patron of the World Conservation Union and the Landmine Survivors Network, and serves on the Boards of the World Wildlife Fund, Seeds of Peace, and the International Commission on Missing Persons. Her Majesty is recognized as a humanitarian activist for issues including the environment, refugees, education, and peace-building in the Middle East and throughout the world.

PETER A. SELIGMANN, U.S.A.
Peter A. Seligmann is co-founder, chairman, and C.E.O. of Conservation International and has worked professionally in environmental conservation since 1976. Under Mr. Seligmann's leadership, Conservation International works around the globe protecting remaining wilderness areas and biodiversity hotspots by demonstrating that people and nature can live in harmony.

MAURICE STRONG, CANADA
Maurice Strong is special advisor to the Secretary-General of the United Nations, president of the Council of the University for Peace, and chairman of the Earth Council. He was secretary-general of the United Nations Conference on the Human Environment held in Stockholm in 1972, as well as of the United Nations Conference on Environment and Development held in Rio de Janeiro in 1992. He has received honorary doctorates from 49 universities worldwide.

ALICE WATERS, U.S.A.
Alice Waters is chef and owner of Chez Panisse restaurant in Berkeley, California. Over the past three decades, Chez Panisse has cultivated a network of local farmers who share the restaurant's commitment to sustainable agriculture. In 2001, Chez Panisse was named best restaurant in the United States by *Gourmet* magazine. She is author of eight books, the most recent of which is *Chez Panisse Fruit* (HarperCollins, 2002).

DR. KEN YEANG, U.K. / MALAYSIA
Dr. Ken Yeang is an architect with offices in London, Kuala Lumpur, and Beijing. His firm, Hamzah & Yeang, specializes in the ecological design of large buildings and sites. His recent books include *The Green Skyscraper* (Prestel, 1999) and *A Vertical Theory for Urban Design* (John Wiley and Sons, 2002).

_ **MAGNUM** PHOTOGRAPHERS

ABBAS was born in Iran in 1944. He joined Magnum in 1985 and resides in Paris. His main subjects include Christianity, Iran, Islam, Mexico, and the Third World.

MICHA BAR-AM was born in Berlin in 1930. He became a Magnum correspondent in 1976 and resides in Ramat Gan, Israel. His main subjects include Israel and Jordan.

BRUNO BARBEY was born in Morocco in 1941. He joined Magnum in 1968 and resides in Paris. His main subjects include Asia, Italy, Morocco, Nigeria, Poland, and Portugal.

IAN BERRY was born in England in 1934. He joined Magnum in 1967 and resides in London. His main subjects include East Asia, the English, and South Africa.

MIGUEL RIO BRANCO was born in the Canary Islands in 1946. He became a Magnum contributor in 1976 and resides in Brazil. His main subjects include Bahia, boxers, and Brazil.

RENÉ BURRI was born in Switzerland in 1933. He joined Magnum in 1959 and resides in Paris and Zurich. His main subjects include Che Guevara, China, Cuba, the Germans, the architecture of Le Corbusier, the Middle East, and Picasso.

CHIEN-CHI CHANG was born in Taiwan in 1961. He was nominated to Magnum in 1995 and resides in Baltimore. His main subjects include Chinatown, New York, and Taiwan.

BRUCE DAVIDSON was born in the United States in 1933. He joined Magnum in 1959 and resides in New York. His main subjects include Brooklyn gangs, Central Park, East 100th Street in New York, New York harbor, and the New York subway.

LUC DELAHAYE was born in France in 1962. He joined Magnum in 1998 and resides in Paris. His main subjects include Afghanistan, Chechnya, Croatia, Haiti, portraits, and Rwanda.

RAYMOND DEPARDON was born in France in 1942. He joined Magnum in 1979 and resides in Paris. His main subjects include Africa, Chad, Chile, cinema, France, and the San Clemente Psychiatric Hospital.

THOMAS DWORZAK was born in Germany in 1972. He became a Magnum nominee in 2000 and resides in Moscow. His main subjects include the war in Chechnya, the evacuation of Grozny, and life in the Caucasus.

NIKOS ECONOMOPOULOS was born in Greece in 1953. He joined Magnum in 1994 and resides in Preveza. His main subjects include the Balkans, Greece, Orthodox religion, and Turkey.

ELLIOTT ERWITT was born in the United States in 1928. He joined Magnum in 1954 and resides in New York. His main subjects include American architecture, beaches, dogs, eastern Europe, and museums.

MARTINE FRANCK was born in Belgium in 1938. She joined Magnum in 1983 and resides in Paris. Her main subjects include the elderly, landscapes, portraits, the Théâtre du Soleil, Tory Island, and Tulkus.

STUART FRANKLIN was born in England in 1956. He joined Magnum in 1990 and resides in Oxford. His main subjects include environment, megacities, Mexico, and Tiananmen Square.

JEAN GAUMY was born in France in 1948. He joined Magnum in 1986 and resides in Normandy. His main subjects include farmers, fishing, French prisons, Iran, and Normandy Bridge.

BRUCE GILDEN was born in the United States in 1946. He was nominated to Magnum in 1998 and resides in New York and Paris. His main subjects include France, Haiti, Ireland, Japan, and street portraits in New York.

BURT GLINN was born in the United States in 1925. He joined Magnum in 1954 and resides in New York. His main subjects include Japan, Russians, and the U.S.A.

HARRY GRUYAERT was born in Belgium in 1941. He joined Magnum in 1986 and resides in Paris. His main subjects include Baie de Somme, Belgium, Egypt, landscape, and Morocco.

DAVID ALAN HARVEY was born in the United States in 1944. He joined Magnum in 1997 and resides in Washington, D.C. His main subjects include America's Atlantic islands, Cuba, Latin America, and the Maya.

THOMAS HOEPKER was born in Germany in 1936. He joined Magnum in 1989 and resides in New York. His main subjects include East Germany, the Maya, New York, and Vienna.

DAVID HURN was born in England in 1934. He joined Magnum in 1965 and resides in South Wales. His main subjects include Arizona, the Hungarian Revolution, and Wales.

CARL DE KEYZER was born in Belgium in 1958. He joined Magnum in 1990 and resides in Ghent. His main subjects include eastern Europe, India, religion in the U.S.A., and Russia.

JOSEPH KOUDELKA was born in Czechoslovakia in 1938. He joined Magnum in 1971 and resides in Paris and Prague. His main subjects include exiles, Gypsies, pollution, the Soviet invasion of Prague in 1968, and urban and rural landscapes.

HIROJI KUBOTA was born in Japan in 1939. He joined Magnum in 1970 and resides in Tokyo. His main subjects include China, North Korea, and the U.S.A.

PAUL LOWE was born in England in 1963. He joined Magnum in 1993 and resides in London. His main subjects include the war in Chechnya, post-Soviet eastern Europe, Rwanda, and Somalia.

CONSTANTINE MANOS was born in the United States in 1934. He joined Magnum in 1965 and resides in Boston. His main subjects include American color, Bostonians, Greece, and music.

PETER MARLOW was born in England in 1952. He joined Magnum in 1986 and resides in London. His main subjects include Tony Blair, landscapes, Liverpool, London by night, and Spain.

FRED MAYER was born in Lucerne in 1933. He joined Magnum in 1989 and resides in Zurich. His main subjects include London, Paris, the Vatican, Jerusalem, the river Jordan, threatened peoples and civilizations, and Chinese opera.

STEVEN McCURRY was born in the United States in 1950. He joined Magnum in 1993 and resides in New York. His main subjects include Afghanistan, Burma, India, Kuwait, portraits, and Sri Lanka.

INGE MORATH was born in Austria in 1923 and died in 2002. She joined Magnum in 1955. Her main subjects included China, country life, the Danube, Iran, Pamplona, portraits, Russia, Spain, Tunisia, and Venice.

JAMES NACHTWEY was born in the United States in 1948. He joined Magnum in 1989 and resides in New York. His main subjects include Afghanistan, Asia, Gaza, Lebanon, Rwanda, and war and social conflict in El Salvador.

MARTIN PARR was born in England in 1952. He joined Magnum in 1994 and resides in Bristol. His main subjects include bad weather, bored couples, the British middle class, food, and tourism.

GILLES PERESS was born in France in 1946. He joined Magnum in 1974 and resides in New York. His main subjects include Bosnia, the conflicts in Northern Ireland, Hebron, following the footsteps of Simon Bolivar, Iran, and Rwanda.

GUEORGUI PINKHASSOV was born in Russia in 1952. He joined Magnum in 1994 and resides in Paris. His main subjects include Japan, La Défense de Paris, and Russia.

FERDINANDO SCIANNA was born in Italy in 1943. He joined Magnum in 1989 and resides in Milan. His main subjects include fashion, the Kami community in Bolivia, landscapes, Lourdes, portraits, and Sicily.

CHRIS STEELE-PERKINS was born in Burma in 1947. He joined Magnum in 1983 and resides in London. His main subjects include Afghanistan, Africa, Beirut, Britain's inner cities, London, and teddy boys.

DENNIS STOCK was born in the United States in 1928. He joined Magnum in 1957 and resides in Woodstock, NY. His main subjects include Alaska, California, James Dean, flowers, France, Japan, jazz, New England, Provence, the U.S.A., and U.S. national parks.

LARRY TOWELL was born in Canada in 1953. He joined Magnum in 1993 and resides in Ontario. His main subjects include El Salvador, family photographs, Gaza, the Mennonites, and Mexico.

ALEX WEBB was born in the United States in 1952. He joined Magnum in 1979 and resides in New York. His main subjects include the Amazon, Florida, Haiti, Mexico, and the tropics.

DONOVAN WYLIE was born in Northern Ireland in 1971. He joined Magnum in 1997 and resides in London. His main subjects include Ireland, Moscow, and travelers.

PATRICK ZACHMANN was born in France in 1955. He joined Magnum in 1990 and resides in Paris. His main subjects include the Chinese diaspora, immigration in Marseilles, Jewish identity in France, the mafia, Malians, motorway landscapes, and the Beijing student uprising.

_ INDEPENDENT PHOTOGRAPHERS

DANNIELLE HAYES was born in Canada in 1943. She is a freelance photographer and resides in New York and Vancouver. Her main subjects include travel, sustainable development, international organizations, Canada, Africa, Latin America, and Asia.

TIMOTHY HURSLEY was born in the United States in 1955. He resides in Little Rock, Arkansas. He began photographing contemporary architecture in 1980. He is the coauthor of *Rural Studio: Samuel Mockbee and an Architecture of Decency*.

SARAH OEHL was born in the United States in 1977. She is a freelance photographer and resides in New York. Her main subjects include family, portraits, and young women.

JARRET SCHECTER was born in the United States in 1963. He is a freelance photographer and resides in New York. His main subjects include people, community, and worldwide sustainable development.

FACT REFERENCES

PAGE 14 Nierenberg, Danielle. "Migrants and Refugees on the Move." *Vital Signs 2001*. Publications of the Worldwatch Institute (New York: W. W. Norton & Company, 2001): 143.

PAGE 19 Engelman, Robert, Brian Halweil, and Danielle Nierenberg. "Rethinking Population, Improving Lives." *State of the World 2002*. Publications of the Worldwatch Institute (New York: W. W. Norton & Company, 2002): 134.

PAGE 24 Taylor, Allyn L., and Douglas W. Bettcher. "WHO Framework Convention on Tobacco Control: A Global 'Good' for Public Health." *Bulletin of the World Health Organization* (Geneva: July 2000): 923.

PAGE 29 UNICEF, <http://www.unicef.org/specialsession/press/fastfacts.htm>, viewed 23 May 2002.

PAGE 45 Watson, Robert T. Climate Change 2001, presented at the Sixth Conference of the Parties to the United Nations Framework Convention on Climate Change, 19 July 2001, at <http://www.ipcc.ch/press/COP6.5/COP-6-bis.htm>, viewed 23 May 2002.

PAGE 52 Sierra Club, <http://www.sierraclub.org/population/factsheets/biodiversity.asp>, viewed 20 May 2002.

PAGE 60 World Water Vision. "World's Rivers in Crisis: Some Are Dying; Others Could Die." Press release. Washington, D.C.: World Water Council, 29 November 1999.

PAGE 66 United Nations Environment Program. *Global Environment Outlook 3* (London: Earthscan Publications, 2002).

PAGE 72 U.S. Department of Energy, <http://www.eren.doe.gov/buildings/consumer_information/refrig/refwhy.html>, viewed 24 May 2002.

PAGE 78 Brown, Lester. "New York: Garbage Capital of the World." *Eco-Economy Updates* (Washington, D.C.: Earth Policy Institute, 17 April 2002): 6.

PAGE 80 Green Roofs for Healthy Cities, <http://www.peck.ca/grhcc/about.htm>, viewed 22 May 2002.

PAGE 93 International Bamboo Foundation, <kauai.net/bambooweb/whybamboo.html>, viewed 20 May 2002.

PAGE 101 Gardner, Gary, and Brian Halweil. "Overfed and Underfed: The Global Epidemic of Malnutrition." *Worldwatch Paper 150*. U.S.A.: Worldwatch Institute, 2000.

PAGE 104 DeVore, Brian. "Hog Heaven." *Yes! A Journal of Positive Futures 14* (summer 2000): 23.

PAGE 108 Organic Consumers Association, <www.organicconsumers.org>, viewed 28 May 2002.

PAGE 114 Schlosser, Eric. *Fast Food Nation: The Dark Side of the All-American Meal*. (New York: Houghton Mifflin Company, 2001): 4.

PAGE 117 Ackerman, Jennifer. "Food: How Safe? How Altered." *National Geographic*, May 2002, 37.

PAGE 122 U.S. Dept. of Education, <www.ed.gov/americareads/sum_TV.doc>, viewed 3 June 2002.

PAGE 135 Tupperware, 2002.

PAGE 138 UNESCO, <http://www.unesco.org/education/esd/english/activities/media.shtml>, viewed 23 May 2002.
Huvane, Kathleen. "Teacher Shortages Hit Hard." *Vital Signs 2002*. Publications of the Worldwatch Institute (New York: W. W. Norton & Company, 2002): 154.

PAGE 147 Sampat, Payal. "World's Many Languages Disappearing." *Vital Signs 2001*. Publications of the Worldwatch Institute (New York: W. W. Norton & Company, 2001): 144.

PAGE 152 Joint United Nations Programme on HIV/AIDS. *AIDS Epidemic Update*. (Geneva: UNAIDS/WHO, December 2001): 1.

PAGE 157 United Nations Children's Fund. *Sanitation for All: Promoting Dignity and Human Rights*. New York: UNICEF, 2000.

PAGE 165 FAO, IFAD, WFP. *Reducing Poverty and Hunger: The Critical Role of Financing for Food, Agriculture and Rural Development*. Paper prepared for the International Conference for Financing and Development (Monterrey, Mexico, 2002): 3.

PAGE 166 United Nations High Commission for Refugees, <www.unhcr.ch/cgibin/texis/vtx/home?page=statistics>, viewed 21 May 2002.

PAGE 169 Deen, Thalif. "Trafficking in Humans Reprehensible, Says Annan." *IPS Terra Viva*, 14 December 2000.

PAGE 172 Visualizing Earth UCSD, <visearth.ucsd.edu/VisE_Int/aralsea/>, viewed 23 May 2002.

PAGE 178 Veenhoven, Ruut. "What We Know About Happiness." Paper presented at the dialogue on "Gross National Happiness" (Woudschoten, Zeist, The Netherlands, January 14–15, 2001): 7.

PAGE 184 People & the Planet, <www.peopleandplanet.net/doc.php?id=1114>, viewed 24 April 2002.

PAGE 191 People & the Planet, <www.peopleandplanet.net/doc.php?id=1115>, viewed 24 April 2002.

PAGE 193 Fédération Internationale de Football Association, <http://www.fifa.com/fifa/survey_E.html>, viewed 21 May 2002.

PAGE 198 People & the Planet, <www.peopleandplanet.net/doc.php?id=1117>, viewed 24 April 2002.

PAGE 208 Nierenberg, Danielle. "Migrants and Refugees on the Move." *Vital Signs 2001*. Publications of the Worldwatch Institute (New York: W. W. Norton & Company, 2001): 143.

PAGE 212 Mattel Inc., 2000

PAGE 215 SustainableBusiness.com, <sustainablebusiness.com/newsletter/index.cfm#prog>, viewed 23 May 2002.

PAGE 221 International Institute for Environment and Development, vol. 3, *The Future Is Now* (London, May 2002): 2.

PAGE 222 SustainableBusiness.com, <sustainablebusiness.com/newsletter/index.cfm#prog>, viewed 23 May 2002.

PAGE 227 Sampat, Payal. "Internet Continues Meteoric Rise." *Vital Signs 2002*. Publications of the Worldwatch Institute (New York: W. W. Norton & Company, 2002): 82.
Sheehan, Molly O. "Mobile Phone nUse Booms." *Vital Signs 2002*. Publications of the Worldwatch Institute (New York: W. W. Norton & Company, 2002): 84.

PAGE 231 Barrett, Amy, and Michael Arndt. "Can Pfizer Stay This Robust?" *BusinessWeek Online*, 18 March 2002.
Halweil, Brian. "Pharmaceutical Sales Thriving." *Vital Signs 2001*. Publications of the Worldwatch Institute (New York: W. W. Norton & Company, 2001): 106.

PAGE 238 Resource Renewal Institute, <www.rri.org/envatlas/europe/netherlands/nl-index.html>, viewed 22 May 2002.

PAGE 246 Pennsylvania Department of Environmental Protection, <http://www.dep.state.pa.us/dep/deputate/airwaste/wm/recycle/FACTS/benefits4.htm>, viewed 24 May 2002.

PAGE 251 Flavin, Christopher. "Wind Energy Surges." *Vital Signs 2002*. Publications of the Worldwatch Institute (New York: W. W. Norton & Company, 2002): 42.

PAGE 261 Brown, Lester R. *Eco-Economy: Building an Economy for the Earth* (New York: W. W. Norton & Company, 2001): 199–200.

PHOTO REFERENCES

CREDITS

OUR WORLD IN FOCUS: MOVING TOWARD A SUSTAINABLE FUTURE
is a project of the Earth Pledge Foundation.

Publisher Vision On Publishing
Design Buero New York
Project | Production Director Francesca Sorrenti
Project Director Marisha Shibuya
Photography Editor Francesca Sorrenti
Editors Mindy Fox / Marisha Shibuya
Assistant Editors Tamar Hahn / Cathy Lang Ho
Media Designer Heather Sommerfield
Editorial | Production Assistant Sarah Oehl
Copy Editor Judith Sonntag

Earth Pledge Foundation
122 East 38th Street
New York, NY 10016
tel: (212) 725-6611
fax: (212) 725-6774
www.earthpledge.org

President Theodore W. Kheel
Executive Director Leslie Hoffman

ACKNOWLEDGMENTS

EARTH PLEDGE FOUNDATION WISHES TO EXPRESS SPECIAL THANKS TO THE FOLLOWING INDIVIDUALS AND ORGANIZATIONS:

To Francesca Sorrenti, Marisha Shibuya, and Jarret Schecter, who turned the concept into reality.

To all the Magnum photographers whose artistry illustrates these pages and to the independent photographers: Dannielle Hayes, Timothy Hursley, Sarah Oehl, and Jarret Schecter.

To the contributors who generously shared their knowledge: Beatrice Biira, His Holiness the Dalai Lama, Nitin Desai, John Elkington, Thomas E. Lovejoy, Her Majesty Queen Noor, Peter A. Seligmann, Maurice Strong, Alice Waters, and Ken Yeang.

To the Buero New York design team: Alex Wiederin, Sylvia Gruber, Seth Hodes, and Erick Ruales.

To the following individuals in recognition of their assistance: David Strettell, Lodi Gyari, Hemanta Mishra, Tufan Kolan, Kevin Kelley, Elana Berkowitz, Cameron Kane, Ian Wolff, Ashok Khosla, Jan-Gustav Strandenaes, Rosalee Sinn, Kate Mhlanga, Gani Serrano, Joan Martin-Brown, Barbara Pyle, Christian de Laet, Wayne Kines, Hiro Shibuya, Heike Leitschuh-Fecht, and the Earth Pledge staff.

And to the following organizations, which have kindly opened their doors to our photographers: Organisation for Industrial, Spiritual, and Cultural Advancement (OISCA), Japan; Population and Community Development Association, Thailand; Development Alternatives, India; Family of Disabled, India; Heifer Project International, U.S.A., Burkina Faso, and Mali; Helen Keller Worldwide, U.S.A.; Helen Keller International, Burkina Faso and Mali; Trickle Up, U.S.A.; Call A Bike, Germany; Hermannsdorfer Landwerkstätten Foundation, Germany; United Nations Development Program, Senegal; Africa 2000, Senegal. Retouching by Hound Dog, U.S.A.